A Father's Advice to Son

Creates the RAMP Solution

A Father's Advice To Son

Creates the RAMP Solution

BY

CARLO FREEMAN

NOTICE

This book is for entertainment purposes only. This book is not meant to provide health care, nor is this medical advice. See a medical professional if you are seeking health care advice. This book is not meant to diagnose or to treat medical conditions. The author takes no responsibility for any actions you take from reading this book.

If you suspect you are suffering from mental problems such as addiction or any other medical condition, please seek help from a qualified medical professional. This book is not written by a medical professional.

TABLE OF CONTENTS

FOREWORD

Read this book as fiction. One should read this book as a father writing to a child. This book is the advice of a father to quite the annoying habit of watching pornography and masturbation. I cannot stress enough that if you are suffering from an addiction or a compulsion that is seriously affecting your life, then this is not the book for you. Instead, seek medical advice from a trained medical professional.

As stated in the title of this book, this is the account of one man's journey to stop viewing pornography. This book contains the program I followed backed by the research that I could find. I make no claims that this book will be your solution. I am not a health care professional. This book is my research, my notes, my journal, and my conclusions. This book is for entertainment purposes. Any strategies or activities you decide to adopt, you do at your own risk. Again, this book is not written by a medical professional but by someone who personally struggled with the annoying habit. This book is the advice I would give my child if he/she was struggling with pornography and masturbation.

This book includes references to medical journals and other material written by medical professionals. These references give you the option to read sources that are written by medical professionals and draw your conclusions. This book includes interpretations and conclusions made from those references that are made by me, a non-professional.

Additionally, know that the vast majority of references and citations made in this book will come from the study and research done about addiction. As you can probably imagine, there is much more research about addiction than compulsions or annoying habits. This book speculates that the brain acts similarly to annoying habits as it does to addiction. This book speculates that references to addiction will help better understand this compulsion for adult images. However, in no way should a reader conclude that this book would be adequate to treat addiction or a serious compulsion. As mentioned above, if you are suffering from an addiction or a serious compulsion, you should seek the help of a medical professional, which will most likely be in the form of a psychiatrist or a psychologist.

With that said, I am happy with the information contained in this book. If one of my children ever struggles with this annoying habit, the ideas in this book are what I would share. And only if the habit was more of an annoyance for that child rather than an addiction or a serious compulsion that was seriously affecting the child's life. If it were the latter, I would seek immediate professional help from the medical community.

This book will call the annoying habit an addiction. Calling it an addiction is down out of exaggeration and artistic licence. It is also done to keep parity with this book and the research that is available. The idea is to treat something to be more serious than it really is so that adequate effort is given to beat the annoying habit. In no way, should the exaggerations in this book, of calling an annoying habit an addiction, lead one to think this book is adequate to treat a serious medical condition such as addiction.

PREFACE

The brain was born without addictions; its natural state is to be without addictions. The brain wants to heal so that it is without addiction. You may be surprised at how easy it is to beat the addiction once you know the rules of this game and how it works in your mind. The brain will work with you to heal itself. Just like if you have ever suffered a broken bone. The body wants to heal and will do so if you give the bone a chance to heal. Give your body the right conditions and the body heals on its own.

The addiction is not as hard to beat as we make it seem. It is the lack of understanding of how the brain works and how the addiction functions that make it seem as if the addiction is difficult to beat. This book will tell you how the game is being played in your mind and then give you strategies and activities to work with the natural tendencies of the mind to then allow the mind to heal itself.

I am excited to share this information with you. I have done my best to take the ideas that I have researched and transformed them into something easy to understand and, more importantly, easy to follow. This book was designed to be concise and to the point. However, this book will repeat some concepts as an emphasis on their importance (you probably already notice the repetition already made with this book not providing medical advice). The idea is to give you all the information you need and to get you started on the program as quickly as possible. A lengthy and overly technical book should not be another hurdle that you must overcome to quit this addiction. Ideally, this book would be read during a weekend and then put into practice the following week. The quicker you can start the program, the quicker you'll create the life you were meant to live.

I struggled with the addiction for a decade and a half. My addiction began in my teen years. Statistically, it is much easier to form addiction in the teen years. [1] For most readers, you will probably be able to relate to my experience of forming the addiction during your teen years.

While in my early 20's and struggling with the addiction, I had the unique opportunity to have severely limited internet access for 2 years. This experience allowed me to experience what life would be like without the addiction. However, as I painfully discovered when I returned to my "normal" life, complete with internet access, I quickly returned to my addiction. Returning to the addiction caused me significant regret in knowing the way I should be feeling as compared to what life is like with the addiction. At the time, I had no idea that this regret was part of the reason why the addiction came back so quickly.

Around 6 years after returning to my addiction, I finally sought help. The help was expensive and incomplete. There was quite a bit that I still had to figure out on my own. Now I want to add my experience and what worked for me into this book. I want to give you an affordable, easy to follow, and concise program to help you quit the addiction.

I now have a life that is free from pornography and masturbation. There is no comparison between life with addiction and life as a free man. Words care not sufficient to express the difference between these two lives. So briefly, I will say that for me, the most noticeable difference is confidence, especially when interacting with women. Along with confidence is overall satisfaction with whatever life gives me. Additionally, freedom has meant an increase in energy and an ability to enjoy the simple joys of life. I am now living the life I was meant to live.

I want to stress that becoming addiction free is worth all the effort that it takes to get there.

As stated above, I am not a medical professional. However, it should be noted that most people who quit an addiction do so on their own. We can only guess the percentage of people who quit on their own since the people who develop and quit an addiction do so quietly without help from a medical professional or group meetings. An estimate would be that 2 to 3 times the amount of people recover from addiction on their own than compared with those who seek help. These people are called "natural recoverers" by the medical community. [2] If those are the estimate statistics for addiction, imagine how those statistics must look for those with an annoying habit. I want to share my ideas and thoughts about addictions so that you might gain a new perspective and gain some insight into how I was able to quit. I intend that after reading this book, you will have the knowledge and encouragement to be one of the many "natural recoverers."

In that effort, this book was written to share precise strategies and activities to help you win your battle against this addiction. Stay consistent and do not quit until you achieve recovery, even if that means that you seek medical help.

Please note that I have used information and research about addictions in general, and I am applying them to this annoying habit. The idea is that addictions are somewhat like an oversized annoying habit. There is a loss of control, but that loss does not reach the level of addiction. It is only an assumption that the mechanisms in the brain that create annoying habits will be very similar if not the same mechanisms that create addictions. I hope that if I took our understanding of addiction and then applied them to this annoying habit, then it would be like using the techniques used to capture a lion to capture a wild cat instead. While the techniques may be overkill, the result should be a satisfactory one.

Throughout the rest of this book, you will hear the term addiction used to describe this compulsion. Again, if you are suffering from addiction, you should seek professional medical help, which this book is not. Please enjoy the read. I thank you for this opportunity to share my research and my ideas with you. These are just my ideas that I would share with my son if he asked me for advice.

CHAPTER 1: FUNDAMENTALS

The Purpose of this Book

This book is designed to give you everything you need to quit the addiction to viewing pornography and masturbation. This book will teach you about your brain and then give you strategies and activities to heal your brain. Once you understand how your brain functions, you will better understand why the strategies and activities contained herein will help you heal. By healing the brain, you will cure the addiction. The truth is your problem has nothing to do with pornography or masturbation but instead has everything to do with chemicals created in the brain. **The brain is not addicted to pornography but instead to brain chemicals.** Heal the brain, and you cure the addiction. What we will create is a healed brain that does not need the brain chemicals that are produced by the addiction.

You may read topics that you do not agree with completely, and that is okay. This book will make some assumptions without having evidence to support it. One assumption is to call our problem an addiction, while professionals in the field may prefer the term "compulsion." This book will make a leap of faith and call this problem an addiction. [3] Not only will it classify it as an addiction but will also make another leap of faith and assume that this addiction is very similar to other addiction, including substance abuse addictions. I think many may agree that this addiction to adult material is more than just a compulsion, and there truly is a loss of the ability to stop. The assumption is that by using research from all types of addictions and how it affects the brain, that there is more benefit than drawbacks. Many addiction professionals are beginning to theorize that all addictions are the same and that the substance or activity that causes the addiction plays a less important role in characterizing addiction. [2]

The key takeaway is to understand how your brain functions and how to work with your brain to help it heal. We want to keep a focus on the bigger picture and not get caught up in details. Don't get caught up in minor details so that you can't see the forest for the trees as the cliché goes. Take what you can get and use the tools you think will work for you. It's okay to tailor the program to what you connect with most. However, some activities are crucial to your success. These activities are heavily stressed as necessary. Additionally, it would be helpful to read this book multiple times during your recovery. I think you'll see that certain ideas presented in this book will mean more to you during different stages of your recovery.

I also want to ask, or at least prepare you, that some of the ideas in this book may be offensive. Please do not take offense and know that it is not my intention. If you find something offensive or disagreeable, please ignore the offense and focus on what is agreeable to you. You don't need to agree with the entirety of this book to gain value from it.

Men as Target Audience

The audience for this book is primarily men and, more specifically, young men. This focus is because one estimate showed that 87% of men aged 18 to 26 reported using pornography, with only 31%

of females in the same age group claiming the same. [4] However, women can use this book and achieve success. Just understand that this book is from the male perspective. It certainly will not be difficult to change the meaning internally for a female's perspective. Just note if you are a woman using this book that there may be more of a stigma put on you by society. This stigma may heighten some of the feelings of "regret" and other emotions that may reinforce the addiction. [5] These feelings will be discussed in more detail in the next chapter.

Excuses

Men, in general, have made excuses for their addiction. I hope after reading this book, you will feel confident that these excuses are merely that, excuses. They have no validity and except to take responsibility away from overcoming the addiction. Excuses allow someone to live in denial. Boiling down the plethora of excuses, there are maybe three main excuses that men use, and they are:

1. All men watch pornography.
2. Pornography does not affect me.
3. It is impossible to quit.

Let's talk about these excuses individually.

All Men Watch Pornography

We will talk about the Triple-A Engine of pornography later, which will explain why the internet has allowed so many men to become addicted. While it may be somewhat accurate to say that perhaps every man with internet access has viewed pornography, it is not true that all men develop an addiction or that they are unable to break the addiction. The cliché that "misery loves company" applies to this excuse. It is a way to give in to peer pressure and makes the man feel like it is natural to watch pornography. However, many men are quitting pornography (Check out the Reddit group NoFap). While reading this book, you will understand how the addiction has hijacked the mind and has created an environment in the mind that is unnatural. The addiction is very damaging and is not something natural or something that everyone participates in doing.

Pornography Does Not Affect Me

We will talk about why this addiction affects people at a young age, with the majority starting in their teen years. If someone develops the addiction at such a young age and then carries the addiction into adulthood, how would they know the difference between an addicted brain and a non-addicted brain? In time, they would only have their childhood as a reference point of what it was like to not have an addiction. People tend to disconnect themselves from experiences as a child compared to experiences one has after puberty. They have no reference point to compare what adult life is like without the addiction. It's virtually impossible to compare a life that is free from addiction if all you know is a life with the addiction. This excuse comes from ignorance.

It Is Impossible to Quit

Many of you have probably tried to quit a countless number of times only to fail at each attempt. These failures might lead one to believe that it is impossible to quit and that the addiction is here to stay. When you find other people who have had the same problem of quitting, it only reinforces the idea that it is impossible. The problem is that you do not understand the addiction and how it works in your mind. The only strategy that you have used is willpower. With a clenched fist, men will tell themselves, "Don't look at pornography." Telling your mind not to think about something almost assuredly causes the mind to think about it. In this program, instead of focusing on the addiction, you will be given another focus, which is RAMP. This new focus will shift your attention away from the addiction and gives you a way to work with the mind to focus on positive activities and strategies. This shift in focus allows the mind to heal. We must work with the mechanisms in your mind to create lasting change.

If you are reading this book, then you have not given in to these excuses, and for that, I applaud you. Despite the lies of society, you still believe that you can overcome addiction. This resilience is the attitude that we need to foster, a firm belief that this addiction can have an end.

However, if you are still holding on to excuses, ask yourself, which of these excuses do you use? As you read, this book focuses on the ideas that will give you a new perspective. You need to have a new attitude toward addiction.

During recovery, you will have many challenges. Additionally, an effort is required to experience true recovery. An effort will be needed to keep yourself motivated and consistent with the program. You will need to do activities consistently that help you learn about yourself. If you are still holding on to excuses, you will most likely lack the commitment necessary to achieve full recovery.

Desire: The Number One Determinant of Success

Forced Participants:

I don't know how you got here. And you may be here not by your own will. You might have been given this book through a loved one such as a friend, parent, or spouse (it's embarrassing, but many of us have been there). They may be demanding you to change. I want to tell you that their desire for you to change is not enough. You will, personally, need to desire this change. You've got to do this for you. Ask yourself, how will this change help you in your life? You are going to have to throw aside the resentment and embarrassment that one may feel when someone makes judgments about your life. An easy way to do this is to get a little selfish and find reasons why this change will benefit you. What's in it for you to have an addiction-free life?

If you are reading this book, not by your own choice, you are going to have to reframe the events that brought you here. You must reframe these events in such a way that gives you a desire to be here. This program will most likely fail if you lack desire. [6] To do this, you are going to have to change the story you are telling yourself. This change is called cognitive reframing. If you tell yourself you are being forced to read this, then instinctively, you are going to resist. Resisting opposes desire. You are going to have to change this internal dialog to something much more compelling. Perhaps look deep within yourself and ask yourself, am I at my best when I am acting out this addiction? Do you truly feel fulfilled after acting out this addiction? Perhaps the feelings of shame and sorrow are more accurate. There is probably a part of you that is uncomfortable with this addiction. Focus on that part of you and get a little selfish and start thinking of the benefits you would get from being addiction free. Now you'll need to continue with cognitive reframing and create a new story as to how you got here. Maybe tell yourself that it is the will of God or your internal desires, maybe even your desires on a subconscious level to be addiction-free, that really brought you to this book. The person who brought you this book is a messenger brought to you from God or your subconscious. Create a new story of how you got here that you can eventually believe wholeheartedly. This new story will allow you to have the desire necessary to complete this program.

While this book is designed to give you the tools to cure your addiction, what it cannot do is give you the desire and commitment to follow through with the strategies and activities to heal your mind. The desire to heal will be up to you. There is a price to most things that are desirable in life. Think of anything that you considered to be a worthwhile accomplishment, and there is most likely a price to be paid to achieve whatever it is you are thinking. The same is true with your recovery. There is a price to pay for this freedom, and the price is your commitment. You cannot cheat the process and get results. Currently, no pill will cure you (although soon there may be pills that can assist in recovery. [2]). There are no words or magic spell that can cure you. The thing that will cure you is your ability to do. You must be able to execute the activities in this book. Know that laziness can keep you from getting the life you were meant to have. Also, know that with desire, you will be able to accomplish something that has, most likely, eluded you for years. My promise to you is this: with your desire and your actions, there is nothing on this earth that can stop you from having a non-addicted life.

There is some indefinable element to achievement, a characteristic that does not allow one to give up. I use the words desire and commitment. Maybe it could also be called the human spirit, but there is something deep inside you psychologically that you will awaken if it has not already awakened and caused you to read this book. This human spirit, this desire, and commitment is the number one factor in determining if you will succeed. I cannot give this to you. You have or will awaken this element within yourself. I can only give you encouragement and activities to do so. However, ultimately, it will be you. During this recovery, you will need to pick yourself up dozens of times. Each time you recommit and try again, you will be using this human spirit. Sometimes it is called "chutzpah." Whatever it is, you will need to tap into it.

> *Whether you think you can or whether you think you can't, you're right.*
> *-Henry Ford*

Willing Participants:

Some of you are like I was. Fighting the addiction pretty much from day one. Unfortunately, I did not know who the real enemy was. So, I was fighting the addiction for years and never got to a point where I was able to win. Even after what seemed like countless years of failing, I never gave up hope that it was possible. Some of you are the same. You are here despite what others may have said, "That it is impossible to stop," or "That it is in your nature and that there is nothing wrong with it."

However, you believe that it is possible despite all the personal evidence to the contrary (i.e., the countless failures to quite). This element to achievement, this desire remains alive. I want you to give yourself a moment of pause and reflection. How long have you been fighting this addiction? And yet despite all the countless failures to stop the addiction, you remain hopeful. Is it not incredible that you still believe that you will succeed? There is something incredibly powerful in the person who persists despite countless failures.

To be a "natural recoverer," much of the determination and motivation to follow through will rest on your shoulders. If you want to change your life in any aspect, it will require a certain amount of effort. Procrastinating actions will be detrimental. You have got to do the actions required for change and you must do them promptly, meaning: **do the action now and not later.** Stay consistent with this program. Do what needs to be done. Your mind will work with you to heal itself. All you need is effort and time, and your mind will do the rest.

...the decent program you follow is better than the perfect program that you quit.

-Tim Ferriss

What Have You Lost from the Addiction?

If you say "nothing," you are very much mistaken. This addiction has taken your ability to enjoy life. It may be hard to understand because, as mentioned before, you've probably experienced more of your adult life as being addicted than not being addicted. By adult life, I mean having all the hormones and desires of an adult, life after puberty. There is a certain power that comes with sexual desire, and this addiction takes that power away from us. There is a book called *Think and Grow Rich* by Napoleon Hill. Chapter 11 is entitled "The Mystery of Sex Transmutation." I recommend that you read that chapter. It describes the power that can be harnessed from using your sexuality as a driving force in whatever endeavor you choose in life. From that book:

> *A river may be dammed, and its water controlled for a time, but eventually, it will force an outlet. The same is true of the emotion of sex. It may be submerged and controlled for a time, but its very nature causes it to be ever seeking means of expression. If it is not transmuted into some creative effort it will find a less worthy outlet.*

For us, we, unfortunately, know what that less worthy outlet is. We have lost many hours of intense focus to this less worthy outlet. However, give this program the necessary time, and you can stop the endless hours. Not only can you stop the time waste but, also, you gain creativity and enjoyment for pursuits that are worth your time and energy. This newly found energy will spill over and transform you to be better at family life, church, hobbies, and anything else that requires your attention. You will become incredibly more effective in all your pursuits. Becoming addiction free is worth all the effort that it takes to get there.

What Have You Gained from the Addiction?

We should also recognize that there is something that you gain out of the addiction. Although you may not realize it yet, you do gain something from the addiction. If you've ever had a binge where you've lost hours in one sitting to the addiction, you should realize that this happens because your brain thinks it is gaining something. The brain would not expend that amount of time and energy without a payoff. That payoff was a chemical release that allows you to focus intently on the addiction. This chemical release allowed you to escape all of the troubles you have in real life. While in a binge, the only thing the mind can process is the addiction. All other feelings and worries are cast aside. However, as you know, this is only for a limited time, but for that limited time, an escape from reality is achieved. Make sure to note that it is through a chemical release in the brain (not the adult images).

Imagine if any problem in life that caused you emotional pain could be temporarily solved and in the place of emotional pain was gained pleasure even if for a limited time. Would that not be a scenario that the brain would recognize as beneficial? The brain may even believe that in this limited time of escape may lie the answer to sustained happiness. So, the brain uses any emotional pain as an excuse to escape into the addiction and to experience the brain chemicals that give it a pleasurable release. [7] The brain may even become oversensitive to negative emotions so that even the slightest hint of negative feelings create a powerful urge for the addiction and brain chemicals.

You may have thought that the addiction is based on a desire for sex. There may be some truth to that, but the clear majority (emphasis on majority) of the addiction is based on a desire for brain chemicals. The desire for sex or sex drive plays such a minor role in the addiction that it should be ignored as a cause for the addiction. The brain's wiring for sex is what the addiction takes advantage of, but the desire for sex has little to do with the addiction. Try to make that distinction as soon as possible. Brain chemicals are what the brain is after. And that is evident by binges. Natural lovemaking rarely gets close to the hour mark, and then after orgasm, sexual satiation is achieved (well go into more detail about sexual satiation later). However, if you've had binges that go on for multiple hours were sexual satiation is not achieved, you have a clear sign that this addiction is based on a desire to maintain an artificially heightened level of brain chemicals and not on a desire for sex. We need to make that distinction clear that the desire for brain chemicals is very different from the desire for sex. The desire for sex will motivate you to achieve, while the desire for brain chemicals will motivate you to withdraw from a healthy life.

Try and recognize what you are gaining from this addiction. The answer is an escape from reality. The addiction is the brain's attempt to find lasting happiness in a release of brain chemicals that eventually wear off. The brain has mistaken the euphoria of brain chemicals as a means of achieving lasting happiness. However, the level of brain chemicals released by the addiction is unnatural and cannot be maintained. We must create a new environment where the brain has healthy activities to combat emotional pain. Healthy activities that release brain chemicals within a natural range, within a range that can be maintained and does not create addiction. That is what the RAMP solution aims to do.

Profile of an Addicted Person

There are a couple of attributes that tend to lead someone to be more susceptible to addiction. These characteristics are not "bad," but it is helpful that one recognizes some of the traits that brought on this addiction.

Common traits include:

- Problems dealing with emotions/Ignore emotions [7]
- Devoutly religious/spiritual [8]
- May tend to feel less enjoyment from normal activities [2]

Now, you won't need to change your personality to quit the addiction. However, you will need to tailor your solution so that you work with your natural abilities and give extra effort to where your abilities fall short. You need to know yourself. Notice which of these attributes you would use to describe yourself and be conscious of ways to work with your natural tendency.

Since a good portion of those affected by the addiction will be religious, it worth mentioning that during the discussion of the brain, there will be references made to evolution. This use of evolution is not meant to offend or to deny creation as the origin of man. Hopefully, the religious could concede that God can create man in a process that resembles evolution. That even God would not cheat a process if a process is a perfect way to create man. If there were a process that needed to be followed, God would follow the process with perfection. Nor that this somehow limits God's power. At any rate, please do not be offended or think that a believing in evolution is necessary for this program. Evolution is only used to describe the parts of the brain. It is not necessary to believe in evolution to use this program.

Additionally, if you are not religious, it should be mentioned that there will be references made to religion and scripture references will be made. Just as a belief in evolution is not required, a belief in God is not a requirement for recovery. The process of recovery is not based on religious beliefs, and you will be fine with your current beliefs.

These traits will be mentioned throughout this book. Take a moment and be honest with yourself and analyze yourself. Do you tend to exhibit any of these three traits? Again, these traits are not bad in and of themselves; however, you will learn how these traits need to be recognized and countered with specific actions. Know yourself.

Emotions

If you asked yourself, are emotions real? Many of us may answer "no." You cannot touch an emotion. You cannot hold emotion in the palm of your hand. You can change your emotion by what you focus on, so they are more dynamic than static. And for the most part, society and our upbringing have probably told us, as males, to give less importance to emotions or, at the very least, to not show them in public. Certainly, there is a stigma to a man that cries as compared to a woman that cries.

The solution to addiction does not require you to become more emotional. However, it does require that you give attention to your emotions. You do not need to portray them physical only observe them in your mind. Know how you are feeling. The desire for the addiction (cravings) has a high correlation to certain feelings. Even more than correlation, they are a very likely part of the causation for cravings. [9]

Emotions can be difficult to predict. A person can feel bad at a certain situation while another person may laugh and feel amused by the very same situation. Emotions can seem at times to be random. However, despite the difficulty in predicting which emotions we feel, the creation of emotions goes through a fairly consistent process. First, emotions need a stimulus. That stimulus can be external or internal. It can be something that happens to us, or it can be something that we imagine. Next, we pass judgment on that stimulus and determine where in the spectrum of good or bad does this stimulus lie. The judgment we give to some stimuli may happen instantaneously and without conscious effort. After that judgment is made, then emotion is felt. [10]

For the solution to this addiction, we will focus on the stimulus of emotions to shift our state from emotions that create cravings to emotions that repeal cravings. As the stimulus for emotion can be external or internal, the RAMP solution will first focus on activities that are external and then internal. By creating both external and internal stimuli that are likely to create positive emotions, you will calm your mind and lessen the cravings for the addiction. If you are in a positive mood, it is more likely that you will pass judgment on stimulus in a way that is more beneficial and constructive for you.

The next chapter will discuss the acronym TROUBLED which goes into greater detail of individual emotions that often cause triggers.

Temptation Is Not a Sin

Many of you who are addicted will have a religious background. In most English-speaking countries that religion will be a form of Christianity. [11] I think it is appropriate to clarify that temptation is not a sin. We know from the bible that the devil tempted Jesus. A clear example of this is found in Saint Luke, Chapter 4:2-7, 13. There it talks about Jesus fasting for 40 days, and then he was tempted. Despite the temptation, Jesus remained without sin.

Someone who is addicted will, from time to time, feel an overwhelming urge to seek the addiction, this urge always starts from a trigger. We will talk more about triggers later. The desire to follow through with the addiction is not a sin. Triggers are temptations and are not sins. As you are working through the addiction, you will have many triggers. You should not feel bad about having triggers. Triggers are beneficial because each trigger is an opportunity for you to learn more about yourself and your emotional state. Triggers are calls to action. With time, we will train the brain to not automatically crave the addiction as a false cure to your emotional state or your trigger. With time, the triggers (the rush of craving the addiction) will lessen and then vanish entirely.

Additionally, with the addiction, there is often a feeling of regret or shame after having a slip. A slip means you go through with the addiction. This feeling of regret is often amplified if one is religious. This regret serves a purpose to let you know your values are not aligned with your actions. That who you are deep down is not aligned with what you have done. This emotion is a call to action so that you will not repeat the undesirable action. Unfortunately, with addiction, the choice to not repeat the action is, to some extent, outside of your current abilities, somewhat outside of your control.

I want you to accept that regret is only a call to change future actions. That is all the feeling of regret is trying to accomplish. Regret wants you to commit to lasting change. Regret does not diminish your value to God or those you love. It is merely a beacon calling you to live according to your values.

If you are working on this program and actively doing the strategies and activities, I ask you to minimize this feeling of regret and the shame associated with the addiction. I ask that you calm this feeling of regret by working through the RAMP solution. Complete RAMP every time you have a trigger and convince yourself that you are in the process of aligning your actions with your values. Do not focus on shame and regret while in this program. It is not helpful and is hurtful if you do. If you have problems minimizing the feeling of shame and regret, I suggest that you try affirmations, which we will talk about later.

In many ways, you should welcome triggers as they happen. As you start the program, you will be bombarded by triggers, but as you work through individual triggers and their attached emotions, you will find that certain triggers will reduce in frequency. With time, certain emotions will no longer cause triggers. One day you will notice that you are no longer experiencing triggers. In the meantime, welcome triggers because each trigger is very much an opportunity. Triggers are temptations, and there is no sin in temptation, only an opportunity to learn who you are. Welcome triggers.

> *My brethren, count it all joy when ye fall into divers temptations; Knowing this, that the trying of your faith worketh patience. But let patience have her perfect work, that ye may be perfect and entire, wanting nothing.*
>
> *-James 1:2-4 (King James Version)*

Religion can be a double-edged sword. It is good because it has kept the truth alive inside of you that the addiction can be beaten, but it can keep you in the addiction because of extreme shame and regret. We need to focus on minimizing this shame because it has already served its purpose in convincing you that change is needed. You are now in the process of change, and shame is no longer a priority. You will need to focus on minimizing the feeling of shame as you overcome this addiction.

Use cognitive reframing (the story you tell yourself) to help you shift your focus away from shame and regret. You can tell yourself that God is making you stronger. Each trigger is truly an opportunity to learn about your emotional state. Each trigger is an opportunity that should never be lost. To maximize this opportunity, you must always complete RAMP with each trigger. Use cognitive reframing to feel gratitude for each trigger.

Goal Making

When you make a goal, it is desirable to write it down in definable numbers and give a deadline for its achievement. For those of you that follow these principles of goal making, then to define this goal in numbers would look something like this: the complete elimination of pornography and masturbation from your life with zero instances of an overwhelming desire to watch pornography. The time frame for recovery is 6 months to a year. If you want a solid number, then use 8 months as your deadline. It might take you less, but I want you geared up mentally for the long haul. If you are mentally prepared for a lengthy recovery, you will give yourself the time necessary to notice the changes happening in your brain. These changes often happen gradually and are not noticeable unless you evaluate yourself over longer periods. Additionally, studies have shown that full recovery is more likely as the duration of treatment is increased. [2] So the longer you stick with your self-directed recovery, the more likely you are to achieve recovery.

When you recover from pornography, you are literally changing the shape of your brain. It is truly "mind over matter." This change in the shape of your brain is called neuroplasticity or brain plasticity. Just like building muscle takes time, changing the shape of the brain takes time. So, give yourself time. Also, like muscle building, changes often build on top of themselves gradually. Taking daily inventory is not effective. Instead, take inventory every few weeks or monthly. You are more likely to notice changes over longer intervals of time than over short intervals. Noticing changes is critical when it comes to motivation. Do not cheat yourself from the progress you have made. Take evaluations every couple of weeks or monthly. To take inventory of your progress, you will be asked to keep a journal, which we'll discuss later.

Also, ask yourself how much time have you had this addicted? If you never overcome this addiction, how many more years of life will you spend as an addicted person? How much longer could this addiction continue? In comparison, 8 months is just a drop in the bucket when compared to the time you have experienced addiction or the time that you could stay addicted if you did nothing. If it took 3 or 4 or even 10 times as long, it would still be worth it. How great is it that it is only 8 months?! Think positively and get ready to live the life you were meant to live.

The healing of the brain is progressive. So, you will continually feel better as the addiction is corrected. Every month that goes by on your road to healing will give you greater confidence and greater enjoyment of life. The ability to enjoy the simple pleasures of life will magnify as you cure yourself. Your creative powers will begin to emerge, thus giving you a better ability to enjoy a normal, addiction-free life.

Now, this time frame of 8 months, I make under the assumption that you are older than 25 and addicted for multiple years. If you are younger than 25, you may be able to achieve recovery within a month or two. Anyone under 25 may still be in the prime time for neural plasticity to happen. It will never be easier to create new neural pathways than this period in your life. [12] I wish I was as fortunate as you to beat this addiction at its most vulnerable. If you are in your teens, be as determined as possible to achieve recovery now and avoid years of pain.

Levels of Use

The use of this addiction usually follows a predictable pattern that looks like experimentation, casual use, consistent use, abuse, and then dependence. [2] If you are reading this book, you will probably be on the far end of this scale. Knowing how severe your problem is will most likely be an accurate predictor of how much time and energy you will need to expend to correct the situation. The DSM-IV (Diagnostic and Statistical Manual of Mental Disorders, Fourth Edition) is a manual used by many psychologists. The manual has criteria using a list of symptoms to describe substance dependence and substance abuse.

The symptoms that would classify *substance dependence* include having 3 or more of the following symptoms within 12 months:

1. Developing tolerance defined by increasing dosage to achieve a high or a diminished high from the previous dosage amount.
2. Having withdrawal symptoms that affect you physically, such as anxiety or unable to sleep.
3. Use of the substance increases by the amount or by longer periods than was intended.
4. Unsuccessfully attempting to limit the use or constantly desiring to limit use.
5. Abnormal use of time obtaining, using, or recovering from the effects of the substance.
6. Use of the substance has limited your ability to work, engage with friends, or recreational time.
7. Continue use despite suffering psychological or physical problems from use.

The symptoms that would classify *substance abuse* include having 1 or more of the following symptoms within 12 months:

8. Unable to fulfill duties at work, school, or home.
9. Use of substance at unsuitable settings, thereby creating physically hazardous situations.
10. Legal problems resulting from use
11. Continuing to use a substance despite ongoing personal problems that are caused or made worse by using the substance.

As you can see, these criteria for drug dependence and drug abuse are for drugs. However, the medical community is beginning to classify all addictions as just addiction. The brain reacts to addiction in pretty much the same way as all addictions. [2] With that in mind, we can take the list above and convert dosage to mean the length of time you are viewing or how graphic the images are that you are viewing. By looking at these criteria, probably the majority of readers will find themselves in the abuse category. And that is okay. Accept it and prepare yourself mentally that recovery is going to take some time (probably 8 months), and it is going to take effort on your part to stay consistent with this program.

Please note that in the DSM-5, the next edition to DSM-IV, the categories for addiction will be changing. The categories for addiction will change to "Mild," "Moderate," and "Severe." Where Mild is experiencing two or more of 11 symptoms in 12 months. Moderate is 4 or more. And Severe is 6 or more. Additionally, in the next edition, criteria 10 will change from "legal problems" to "suffering from strong urges and cravings for the addiction." [13]

You can gauge yourself and see where you fall into as far as categories. Do not feel discouraged if you are on the upper end of the spectrum. You can quit the addiction. And for you, the changes in your lifestyle will be even more dramatic than for others. Muster up all the determination you've got to stay consistent with this program.

Rewards and Punishments

In the 1950s, there was a psychologist named B.F. Skinner, who studied behavior. His work showed that positive reinforcements (giving a reward), negative reinforcements (taking away undesirable stimuli), and punishment (giving negative stimuli) could control behavior. [14] This was widely accepted throughout the psychology field. His theories were widely accepted and applied to human behavior. For most of us, our parents raised us with this notion that if you reward an action, you get more of it, and if you punish an action, you get less of it. However, this is not very effective with the addicted mind.

With an addiction, any punishment will generally push the addicted person towards the addiction. It is ineffective to punish an addicted person because their brain will see the punishment as a threat to survival and will seek the comforts of brain chemicals to solve the negative experience. Punishment will tend to reinforce the addiction than diminish it. Therefore, if you are religious, you should not focus on the feeling of regret and shame (remember those feelings are only there so that you change future actions, and that is what you are in the process of doing).

We should focus only on rewards as the way to creating new behaviors and avoid the idea of punishments. You should focus on how your life is getting better and better every day. Focus on positive events in your life and minimize the focus on negative events in your life. This change in focus will help the brain to minimize the cravings for the addiction.

This idea of rewards and punishment is probably deeply ingrained into your thinking even down to the subconscious level. Your parents probably used the ideas of rewards and punishments to encourage good behavior since you were a baby. They maybe gave you a few months grace period after birth because you were such a cute baby, but after that grace period, they started using rewards and punishments to foster good behavior. And this is okay. Using rewards and punishments is responsible parenting, and for the most part, it works. However, for this addiction, you will need to abandon the idea of punishing yourself for triggers and slips. It will not work with addiction. Only rewards will work. It might seem hard for you to accept at first, but please work on changing how you react to your failures when it comes to this particular problem. You will see that the "P" in RAMP is all about rewards.

We are not rewarding slips and triggers, but we are rewarding a new stimulus to create positive emotions and to create natural levels of good brain chemicals.

Types of Supporters

This idea of rewards and punishments spills over to supporters and people in your life. When it comes to a supporter, you will probably have a supporter who is either negative, positive, or an enabler. A negative supporter will try and punish you or belittle you because of your addiction. A positive supporter will encourage you to accomplish your goals. And an enabler will encourage you to stay addicted. If you have a significant other in your life, you can probably guess what type of supporter they will be. You can then choose if you want that person involved in your recovery or not (or to what level of involvement you allow that person to have). It is important to know that you do not have to tell them about your recovery. It might be helpful to do so, but then again, it may not. You can decide whether to involve them in your recovery. Here are some recommendations:

Negative Supporter

If you have a negative supporter, I recommend you do not tell them. Tell them after you have quit the addiction after you have achieved recovery. As the saying goes, it is often easier to ask for forgiveness than to ask for permission. It will be much easier for a negative supporter to allow you to do the things required in this program after the results have been achieved rather than to ask them for understanding while you are in the process of quitting. The negative supporter will probably be more critical of any back steps you have during recovery. This criticism will not be helpful. Additionally, since recovery takes months, they may not have the patience to allow you the time necessary to achieve recovery.

Positive Supporter

If you have a positive supporter, I recommend that you tell them. She has had different life experiences that could be beneficial. Since she has a different perspective than you, she may be able to give you insights into who you are and better connect the dots. This insight will most likely shorten your recovery period. Her insights will be especially helpful if you are someone who tends to ignore emotions. A positive supporter will be more willing to let you do the activities required in this program and may help you find additional activities to support you. She may help you stay motivated and keep you accountable during the many months of recovery. Additionally, working together to achieve recovery would likely create a stronger bond within your relationship.

Enabler

If you have an enabling supporter, I recommend that you separate yourself from that person. If you truly want to quit this addiction, it will probably be best if you cut ties with this person. Otherwise, they will do things to sabotage your progress. It would probably be best to eliminate the person from your life. You can do this nicely to minimize hurt feelings. However, this is probably the best course of action. Again, you will have to be the judge in how much influence this person has on your life.

Probably the most important idea for you to understand is that you created this addiction on your own, and you can quit on your own. You do not have to tell anyone about it if you think it would be too embarrassing or too detrimental to do so. A supporter is not necessary for your recovery. Most people probably have a negative view of pornography. Additionally, there may be a lack of the ability to relate to addiction. Because of that, you may wish to delay disclosing your recovery to others.

A problem that has already been resolved is much easier to handle than something that is still open-ended. First off, the information has a positive ending, which is much easier to accept than simply negative information. For instance, let's say you were doing something silly like practicing your golf swing in the basement. Then you accidentally let the club go, and it brakes a window. If you were to replace the window before anyone got home, it would be much easier to accept what happened. Additionally, it shows others you took ownership of the problem and made an effort to fix it. Delaying the knowledge of the addiction until recovery has been achieved will make it much easier to accept than without having first achieved recovery.

Also, the passing of time can be a pacifier. After you have already achieved recovery, your partner will probably notice that you are more outgoing and more present in the moment. When she asks what has caused the change, that would be a good time to tell her. Tell her you "had" a problem, and now it's over (the problem is already fixed). Next, shift the conversation to your partner. Make this about her. Tell her that you were hoping that she would notice the change. Tell her that part of the reason you did this was for her so that you could truly be yourself. That through recovery, you would be able to know her on a more intimate and personal level. Of course, this not something you should just say but something you should believe. It should be the truth.

Another reason why the passing of time is a pacifier is that the fear of the unknown has been removed. If you tell your partner before you start the program or while in the program, she may question the effectiveness of the program and may become a source of doubt. Doubts are not helpful. Your psychology, whether you believe you can or you believe you cannot, is essential to your ability to complete the program. If you tell the person after the program is completed and your mind has healed. There is no need for doubt. Not only has it worked, but she will see the beneficial results of recovery. The new you will only impress her. And the longer she has been with and enjoyed the new you, the more assured she will be that the problem has been resolved.

Additionally, you should express two main concepts when explaining this addiction to your partner, and they are (1) that it is a mental condition and (2) that you are remorseful. These two concepts will be discussed further in the conclusion of this book.

If you decide to share your addiction and recovery, you should stay positive and slightly excited. Don't make it dramatic or get overly emotional in telling your partner. You will most likely catch her off guard by telling her if she does not already know about your addiction, and since she will be unsure of how to react, she will most likely mirror your emotions. Having an optimistic view of the situation will help her be optimistic, as well.

The True Enemy

This book is meant to give you a path to follow. You need to know who you are and who the enemy is. This book is going to show you who the real enemy is and that it is not pornography. This book is meant to remove the confusion one often feels with addiction. Most of us want desperately to quit the addiction, and the problem is not the "desire" to quit but the "how" to quit. This book will answer the "how" part to quitting the addiction. Then comes the doing part, which is up to you. The doing is in direct relationship to your desire. The more you desire, the easier it is to do the doing.

The true enemy is not pornography. The truth is, you have never been addicted to adult images. The use of the term "pornography addiction" is used to describe the condition, but the reality is pornography has zero importance in the problem or the cure. After reading this book you will understand why pornography is irrelevant. This idea might sound ludicrous; however, consider the reason why you have not been successful in quitting is that you have been fighting something other than the true problem. When you fight pornography, you do nothing to cure the addiction. Rarely, can you focus on something and get less of it. Focusing on not focusing on something is impossible.

You are wasting your time when you fight pornography. **The true enemy is brain chemicals.** Brain chemicals are what the addiction is all about. True, the brain uses pornography to get those brain chemicals. But it is the brain chemicals that the addiction wants. Forget about pornography and focus on healing the brain and reduce harmful brain chemicals. [15] Focus on the brain so that it will not desire an unnatural level of brain chemicals to solve your emotional problems.

Fighting addiction can seem like an impossible cycle. You have probably been able to avoid pornography for a couple of weeks, maybe even for a month; however, the whole time, you are craving the addiction. Without healing the mind, the brain will crave the addiction. It does not matter how much will power you have because eventually, your will power will run out, and you will fail. [16] So, the cycle will continue. You will have a slip. Often these slips could be described as binges where you go all out on the addiction for multiple hours or even days. After your binge, you will feel terrible and then try and quit again by sheer force of will. You last a week or two just to have another binge. Trying to quit the addiction by sheer force of will is a losing man's battle because it does not attack the enemy. The enemy is the brain, more specifically the Limbic System of the brain, which we will discuss in the next chapter.

Unfortunately, for many of us, the only arsenal in our war against the addiction was clenching our fists and trying to use willpower to overcome the addiction. And predictably, this is a failed strategy and a losing battle. It is a failed strategy because many of us try to win the war, that is this addiction, without knowing who the enemy is (brain chemicals are the enemy, not adult images). Without this knowledge, we are destined to fail. This book will teach you about yourself and your brain and then give you strategies and activities to be victorious.

In this book, you will gain many different techniques to use for different situations. These techniques will help you truly win the war against your addiction and claim the Limbic System of your brain as an ally instead of an enemy.

Key Takeaways from the Introduction

1. Excuses for the addiction only excuse a person's responsibility to take action. Excuses are based on facts but ignore the more powerful fact that you have the power to change. Do not use excuses.
2. Desire is the number one determining factor if you will succeed. Desire is up to you to cultivate.
3. The addiction has taken away your enjoyment of life and your creative energy. It is worth overcoming the addiction to get that back.
4. You will have to step outside of your comfort zone when it comes to emotions and take notice of how you are feeling.
5. Temptation and triggers are not sins. They are opportunities to learn about yourself.
6. Pornography is not your problem; brain chemicals are. Make a mental shift to focus on the healing of your brain.
7. This addiction affects mostly men, but women are also susceptible.

8. Changing your brain takes time. Make a goal to be addiction-free in 8 months with the idea that every brain will take a different time frame to heal. Do progress checks over longer periods (each month) versus shorter periods.
9. Focus on rewards rather than punishments. Punishments tend to reinforce the addiction.
10. There are three different types of supporters: positive supporter, negative supporter, and enabler. Decide if you want to include a supporter in your recovery. However, you should know that a supporter is not necessary to recovery.

Chapter 2: The Addiction

It is said that if you know your enemies and know your-self, you will not be imperiled in a hundred battles; if you do not know your enemies but do know yourself, you will win one and lose one; if you do not know your enemies nor yourself, you will be imperiled in every single battle.

-Sun Tzu (Bold added for emphasis)

As stated before, you are not addicted to pornography. I know that seems hard to believe, but it is true. The root of your addiction is brain chemicals. Brain chemicals are the problem and what causes the addiction. You are addicted to brain chemicals. Pornography is just the vehicle the addiction uses to set off the chemical reaction in your brain. You cannot focus on pornography and expect to create changes in your brain. You must focus on the brain to create changes in the brain. Forget about pornography as the problem. Let's start by talking about how the brain became addicted.

Prevalence of Addiction

It is estimated that 28% to 15% of Americans will develop an addiction to alcohol or drugs within their lifetime. Another statistic for nicotine addiction estimates that 24% of Americans will develop an addiction to that substance. We can assume that the people who experience addiction in their lifetime are in the minority, but the experience is hardly unique. It is a common experience that millions of people will experience. [2]

With the research done on addiction, the medical community is treating addiction as a disease. The disposition to developing the disease has much to do with a person's genetics, mental health (including the age at which they begin exposure to the addiction), and the environment in which they live. [2]

Genetics

Observations have been done with twins and families prone to addiction such that it is estimated genetics is responsible for 50% of the risk factor for developing a drug addiction. [2]

Mental Health

Mental health also plays a role in developing an addiction. It is often much easier for someone who is suffering from a mental condition such as depression or anxiety, also to develop a substance addiction to self-medicate. If you are suffering from serious mental health issues, you seek professional medical advice.

Additionally, it is estimated that the brain does not fully develop until around age 25. It is substantially easier for the brain to develop an addiction while still in development (this will be discussed in more detail later). [2]

Environment

Life events can also create a disposition for addiction, such as abuse or neglect, that one experiences as a child can greatly increase the probability of creating an addiction later in life. [2]

There is a certain level of shame that accompanies addiction. This shame will often cause one to hide the addiction from others. You may not know that there are millions of people who are suffering from addiction. Some are people you know. You should not feel alone in this addiction or that you are an outcast. To develop an addiction is quite normal.

There may be characteristics about you that put you in a higher propensity to addiction. You may want to ask yourself which of the above characteristics describe you. Is there a history of addiction in your family? A history of mental health issues? Are there events in the past that cause you emotional pain today? Answering these questions will allow you to focus on certain aspects of this program that will help you deal with those particular issues.

Just to reiterate, if you suffer from severe mental health issues, you will want to seek professional medical help. This book is intended as entertainment and is not written by a medical professional.

It should be noted that the brain wiring that causes addiction is something fundamental to the human brain. The parts of the brain that cause addiction are in every normally developed brain. Anyone, with or without preexisting characteristics of addiction, still can form an addiction. [2] If someone consistently uses the brain wiring for addiction, the neural pathways that cause addiction will form, and that person will develop an addiction regardless if they have a predisposition for addiction or not.

The Triple-A Engine

No generation has had as much exposure to this addition as the most recent generations who grow up with high-speed internet. Since the internet cannot be avoided or stopped (see Why Other Programs Fail: Using Internet Filters), we should instead look inward to ourselves for the solution to the addiction. The solution to this addiction is not external but internal in our own brain. However, it is important to know how the internet has caused so many to experience this addiction. This understanding may alleviate some of the unnecessary blame that we give ourselves, thus reducing the shame and regret of the addiction.

Dr. Al Cooper, a Stanford researcher and clinical psychologist, describes how the internet can affect so many people with this addiction that normally would not become addicted by describing the internet as having a Triple-A Engine. The internet allows a person to develop an addiction through availability, anonymity, and affordability. [17]

Availability

The availability of addiction is a twofold operation.

First, there is availability in the form of practicality. The internet is available in some form to practically every person who has a computer, tablet, or smartphone. This availability allows the addiction to be available on a 24/7 basis. Any moment can become a moment to access the addiction. Availability may be one of the most significant hurdles to overcoming an addiction.

Second, there is a wide variation in the types of genres of pornography available. These different genres of addiction were never widely available to past generations. What makes availability to different genres so dangerous is that it also takes advantage of the Coolidge Effect, which we will discuss later. The generations before us relied more on printed material designed for a wide audience and generally did not cater to specific genres.

If someone exposes themselves long enough to adult material, they will probably find a genre of the addiction that piques their curiosity. This wide variety now available to such a large mass of people has the potential to affect many with this addiction, many who otherwise would not develop a problem.

While we cannot stop the availability of the addiction, however, we can heal our minds. We certainly should not consider ourselves helpless to the addiction. With commitment and effort on our part, we can overcome this addiction.

Anonymity

In past generations, if you wanted access to this addiction, you most likely had to deal with another person, whether it be a store clerk or the mail carrier. This interaction with another person would create a barrier for some people, especially under-aged viewers. Now the average age for a person's first exposure to adult imagery is 11 years old. [18] They are too young to understand what they see and are too embarrassed to talk to their parents. This lack of understanding and embarrassment leads many to form an addiction at an incredibly young age (usually in their teen years). [1]

Additionally, anonymity also allows the viewer to watch genres that otherwise would bring shame to the viewer. Some people think that there is so much anonymity on the internet that they even view illegal forms of graphic material. Some think that there is such a low probability of having their browsing activity monitored that they are willing to take the risk to view illegal forms of material. This false sense of security has allowed some to access genres that they otherwise would never do without the idea of anonymity. It should be noted that your internet provider will not protect your identity if you are viewing illegal forms of material.

Affordability

Older generations could only consume adult material if they were willing to pay for it. This process created a barrier for some people to not even bother with consumption. However, that is no longer the case. The internet has allowed people to develop an addiction for free. No longer is a credit card or a photo identification a barrier to viewing graphic material, again, allowing greater access to under-aged viewers. Also, when money is not an issue, this allows for limitless consumption. This limitless consumption is possible by affordability and by the Coolidge Effect. Additionally, the affordability allows for more anonymity since there is no paper trail of a purchase that could be discovered by a loved one.

In many ways, this addiction is not your fault. It was stumbled upon and through a lack of understanding, became an addiction. In many ways, this addiction was done to you rather than something that you did. It was done by people looking to profit from the addiction. Even though it was done to you, that does not take away your ability to stop this addiction. The ability to stop this addiction is yours. If you have the desire and commitment to follow through with recovery, you can quit this addiction for good.

In sum, the internet has created an environment where a countless number of people who otherwise would not become addicted are now ensnared with this addiction. The answer is not avoiding the internet but learning how to control your brain. The RAMP solution is designed not to avoid the addiction but to work with the brain to allow it to heal. Once the brain heals, the person will then have the ability of a conscious choice and can choose a life without the addiction while maintaining the necessity of internet access.

Parts of the Brain in Conflict

The Limbic System

The brain is not nearly fully understood. Many significant discoveries are being made or reworked. Many significant findings have only recently been discovered. So, we will not get into great detail about the parts of the brain, but we will talk about the two main areas of the brain that cause addiction. These two areas are an overactive Limbic System and a weak Frontal Lobe.

The Limbic System is a somewhat primitive part of the brain. It is believed that this part of the brain is older in the evolution of the brain. Its sole function is to keep you alive. Its location is at the base of the skull. If someone scares you and you jump up in fright, it is the Limbic System that was activated. Or if you start shivering from cold, it is the Limbic System that is causing you to shiver. The Limbic System's main function is to keep you alive. [19] The Limbic System uses chemicals to create emotions. It will release chemicals that help you survive, like adrenaline. It will release pleasurable chemicals in response to actions it wants to create more of, and it will release negative chemicals for actions it wants to limit. All it cares about is keeping you alive in the present moment. It is also responsible for the desire to procreate, which is another form of survival.

The Limbic System's location is at the base of the brain, which means it is a straight shot from the eyes, ears, mouth, and skin. It is the first part of the brain to interpret threats of survival from the senses. So, when something unexpected happens, and you jump in fright, it is the Limbic System that is interpreting information from your senses and reacting to the threat. Then the Limbic System will release adrenaline throughout your body to produce a "fight or flight" response. The Limbic System's location is essential to survival. However, it also means the Limbic System gets first dibs from information received from your sensory systems. It gets to interpret the information from your skin, nose, mouth, ears, and eyes. Most importantly, when it comes to this addiction, it gets first dibs on visual information. When it sees something that is sexually stimulating, it will already start releasing brain chemicals to excite a sexual response. This release is done without the conscious will of the person. It is done before the rest of the brain has a chance to react to visual cues. [20]

Another example of the importance of the Limbic System and its position at the base of the brain is how police snipers will aim for it to produce the instant kill. Snipers will aim for the "apricot," which is the base of the brain. This apricot is the lambic system, and among other things, controls involuntary movement. If you destroy this part of the brain, it is unlikely that the person will survive. And not only will they not survive, but they will have little chance at even involuntary reflexes that are associated with sudden shocks. If you can destroy this part of the brain, there is no chance for survival. So even though the Limbic System might be the source of your addiction, it is a much-needed part of the brain. It has served a very important purpose for thousands of years by keeping humanity alive despite all the dangers Mother Nature imposes.

Along with survival, the Limbic System also cares about rewarding activities that keep you alive. So, if you eat something high in fat, protein, or calories, it is going to reward you with pleasurable chemicals. This reward in the form of brain chemicals is why some people have a strong craving for foods that are not healthy when eaten in large quantities. This reward system also shows that this part of the brain is very old from an evolutionary standpoint. It is one of the first parts of our brain to develop. [19] People who constantly eat foods that are rich in fat and calories become overweight. People who are overweight tend to have a lower life expectancy than those who eat healthier food and maintain healthier body weight.

However, the Limbic System has developed over tens of thousands of years ago during a time when rich foods were not often available. Thousands of years ago people rarely had access to foods that were rich in fat and calories. So, it was a huge advantage to have a brain that rewarded you every time you ate something that was going to keep you alive longer than other foods. If you were able to store some extra fat, you were more likely to live during times of hunger, which often happened thousands of years ago. However, today, this reward wiring is not particularly healthy for us.

Additionally, the Limbic System rewards us for having sex. Sex is the ultimate form of survival. It allows us to carry on half of our genes to the next generation. Having children allows us to, potentially, live on forever, barring any extinction of humans. The Limbic System reserves its most power chemical release for sex, which is the ultimate form of survival. These chemicals are designed to create a desire within us for sex.

Unfortunately, the addiction uses the same reward wiring for sex to cause very powerful chemical releases into your brain. [19] If you are already predisposed to addiction, it will not take much exposure to the addiction to create a desire for more brain chemicals. The addiction fools the Limbic System into thinking it has found the greatest form of procreation ever experienced by man. It thinks it has found the fountain of youth, the Holy Grail, whatever fantastically thing that brings immortality. The Limbic System believes it has found it. And you can bet it is not going to give up this magical gift easily. It wants to hold on to the addiction because it believes it is holding on to immortality.

Of course, just with rich foods, the Limbic System is rewarding something in modern society that will not bring about positive results. It is plausible that people who have an addiction to pornography will be less likely to procreate in real life. Often the addiction is humiliating to those in its grasp and causes a person to withdraw from friends and family and other social functions. Some addicted people will prefer the high of the addiction over the simpler joys of social interaction. Without social interaction and the confidence to interact with women, an addicted person may have less opportunity to have real sexual interactions and less ability to procreate. As this addiction becomes more prevalent in modern society, some people may not have children because of the problems this addiction creates in their life. [21]

The Limbic System works with chemicals to control the brain. Brian chemicals are often associated with emotions. If you think about emotions, they often have a way of getting us not to think. Brain chemicals tend to turn off the higher reasoning abilities of our brain that are based in the Frontal Lobe. If you have ever been in a situation where you thought your life was going to end, often you will have a "fight or flight" moment. The brain will dump adrenaline throughout the body, and this event can happen almost instantaneously and within tenths of a second. If you have had this experience, you know that the brain becomes very focused and usually only capable of thinking of two different scenarios, "fight or flight." Barring any chance at higher reasoning that the brain would normally be able to perform. [21]

If you think of other emotions like feeling sad and depressed, or on the other end of the spectrum, happiness and joy. The emotion seems to have a brain chemical associated with that emotion. It is important to try and note that emotions and brain chemicals tend to go hand in hand. Another example might be someone cutting you off in traffic. There is not only an emotion of rage, but there is something else that you can feel happening in the brain, which is the effects of a chemical release. This chemical will often make it difficult for you to think or shift your focus to something else. This chemical response seems to lock you into the event that just happened, and often, emotion will be felt, such as anger or fear.

Brain chemicals are power. They can shut off higher reasoning. However, in the RAMP solution, you will learn how to quickly recognize a chemical release of the brain and then work with your brain to allow higher reasoning. The RAMP solution will help you keep the Frontal Lobe active and not let it shut down from the chemical release in the brain.

The root of the addiction is that the Limbic System has become overactive. The addiction causes it to believe that any negative emotion is a threat to survival. The Limbic System will respond to any negative emotion with a desire for pleasurable brain chemicals. It believes that the chemicals produced by the addiction can be used to counteract all negative emotions. Even negative emotions that you experience because of the addiction. These negative emotions can create a negative feedback loop that feeds upon itself, which is called the downward spiral, which we will talk about later.

The Limbic System does not know what it is doing. Unfortunately, in today's world, it can sometimes do the opposite of what it thinks it is accomplishing. In today's world, it can reward activities that are detrimental to your overall wellbeing. We need to learn how to calm the Limbic System and be able to keep our higher reasoning intact. Which now brings us to the Frontal Lobe.

The Frontal Lobe

The Frontal Lobe is your greatest ally in the war against addiction. Right now, it is being bombarded by the Limbic System's chemicals, but with some time, you will train the Frontal Lobe to resist the chemicals and then regain functionality.

The Frontal Lobe is the part of the brain that is required for higher reasoning. So, your ability to do math, write, and read will come from this region of the brain. Your electrical thoughts are based in this region of the brain. Your ability to remember the past and make plans for the future comes from the Frontal Lobe.

[22] However, the Frontal Lobe does have receptors and does take in the brain chemicals and is very receptive to those brain chemicals. If the Frontal Lobe is not strengthened, it will bow to the will of those chemicals. The Frontal Lobe will bow to the will of the Limbic System if not strengthened.

While the Limbic System works mainly with brain chemicals to send responses throughout the brain and body, the Frontal Lobe relies more on electrical signals to communicate to the rest of the brain and body. When we think about emotions (fear, anger, sadness, happiness, joy, and surprise), we are often talking about chemical processes in the brain. When we think about thoughts (math, language, engineering, and ideas), we are often talking about an electrical process in the brain. So, in recovery, we will strengthen the electrical signals in the brain and learn how to lessen the effects of the chemical signals in the brain. You can probably predict that keeping track of emotions will be part of that process.

Emotions versus Thoughts

If you think of negative emotions (fear, stress, sadness, and depression), they are all caused by a chemical release in the brain. Take notice of your emotions. When someone cuts you off on the freeway, there is often a very powerful and quick emotional response. However, the opposite of an emotion is a thought. Thoughts are often more associated with figuring out a complex problem. If you think of mathematics or strategies in a board game, you are using thoughts. Thoughts are electrical. They are what make us different from other animals. We need to consider thoughts as superior to emotions. Try to make a distinction between emotions and thoughts. **Through the next couple of days, just take notice of when you are undergoing an emotion that is based on a chemical reaction or when you are going through a thought process that is electrically-based.** There is a different feeling in the brain.

Noticing this difference will allow you to favor thoughts over emotions.

You need to be aware of your emotional state. Favoring thoughts over emotions does not mean to ignore emotions. If you are a person who tends to ignore emotions, you will want to really focus on doing this activity. There is a link between your cravings (triggers) and your emotional state. It's time that you become aware of how you are feeling. You don't need to show these emotions physically, just a conscious realization of your emotions is all we need. After that realization, you will then be free to focus on using thoughts to move towards a better emotional state.

One of the most effective ways to create a shift in your mind, to favor thoughts over emotions, is to monitor and name your emotions. Use your Frontal Lobe to name the emotion to which the Limbic System is responding. If you can say to yourself, "Oh, I am feeling nervous about this test." Naming the emotion "nervous" has a way of minimalizing it. Even better if you can also name the event (in this case, a "test") that is causing the emotion. Take note of the emotion and then analyze it. Ask yourself, "Why am I feeling nervous?" You can use thoughts to come up with a solution to your nervous feeling. Maybe the solution will be to schedule a time to study for the test. After you've used thoughts to come up with a solution, tell yourself you no longer have a reason to feel nervous.

Additionally, if you can think of similar events in your past that you were able to overcome, this will also lessen the emotion. The first step is to monitor your emotions. Then name it. And then analyze what is causing the emotion. Come up with an acceptable solution. Think of past experiences where you were able to achieve a positive outcome.

Sometimes that solution can simply be to accept whatever is causing the emotion as something you have to go through in life.

Accepting the cliché "it is what it is" can be your solution to a problem that you have no power to change.

Using this method of monitoring and naming your emotions is a sure-fire way to create a shift between thoughts and emotions. Use thoughts to analyze emotions. Then name the emotion to own it and minimize its power over you. With time, you will clearly show your subconscious mind that thoughts are superior and to trust thoughts over emotions. Whenever you are working with your subconscious mind, consistency is key to bringing about changes in the subconscious. Stay consistent using your conscious thought to monitor and analyze your emotions.

Just a reminder. Even though we want to favor thoughts over emotions, this does not mean emotions are bad. We do not want to resist emotions. Resisting emotions will tend to make them even more powerful. We do not want to label emotions as bad or good. We simply want to recognize them and name them. Learn to accept all emotions. Even emotions that might be considered "undesirable" are, in reality, good. These emotions are telling us that we should take action in our lives because we perceive a situation that needs to be corrected. Be careful, though, not to take action in the "heat of the moment." We don't want to act inappropriately because of an emotional state instead of a thoughtful state. Accepting and naming emotions helps us move out of an emotional response into a thoughtful response. Also, deep breathing is an incredibly useful tactic for moving out of an emotional response. We will talk about breathing more in the next chapter.

Triggers

A trigger is the moment in which the desire for the addiction begins. This trigger is also known as a craving. It can be difficult in the beginning to notice the moment in which a trigger happens. However, with practice, one can be sensitive and acutely aware of the moment a trigger happens. The easiest way to know that a trigger has happened and that a chemical release has occurred is by noticing an increase in heart rate. With practice, you can feel the slight uptick in heart rate when the Limbic System releases brain chemicals. You can feel a rush of blood as this happens. Triggers are that moment when your mind believes that it will have an opportunity to act out on the addiction.

Triggers have two parts to them:

1. A reminder of the addiction.
2. The emotion state that you are in that makes you susceptible to a trigger. [7]

A reminder of the addiction can be anything from a billboard on the freeway or an attractive girl at school or work. It doesn't have to be visual either. A song on the radio can become a reminder of the addiction. Even random thoughts from the past can cause one to be reminded of the addiction. Which makes triggers much like emotions. The stimuli can be either external or internal. Anything that reminds you of sex can be a reminder of the addiction. Even if you were willing to live in a cave, there would still be a reminder of sex, even if within your mind. You will not be able to control this aspect of triggers. Even though you lack control of what you see and to some extent, what you think about, it is still useful to know how triggers work. Once you see a reminder, you can make a conscious effort to monitor your heart rate. Do you feel a rush of blood? If the answer is "yes," then you are experiencing a trigger (a desire or an urge for the addiction). Remember, the Limbic System has first access to the input of your senses. So, controlling triggers will not be possible in the beginning. You can only monitor yourself and recognize that one has started.

The second part of a trigger is the emotional state you are in when you have a reminder of sex. What is your emotional state at the time you have your reminder of the addiction? This part of a trigger you do have control over. You have near-absolute control over how you feel. Maybe not moment by moment control, but overall, we can determine how we wish to feel.

Often, we allow ourselves to feel a certain way because of the events around us. For instance, if you bought a new sports car and you are cruising around, and people are looking at your new car as you drive around, you might allow yourself to feel satisfaction. You might feel the exhilaration as you slam on the gas and feel the g-forces push you against the seat. However, did the car cause these feelings, or did you allow them to happen? Did the car inject you with endorphins to make you feel great? Of course not, you created that emotion in your brain because you passed judgment on the event, and you thought the event was special. Another example, have you ever kissed a girl and felt exhilaration? Did the girl cause you to feel that way, or did you allow yourself to feel that way because of the circumstances you perceived? The answer to these questions is that you allowed yourself to feel the exhilaration.

You allow yourself to feel the way you do. Your upbringing and experiences have taught you that if "x" and "y" happen, then you get to feel "z." What you need to understand is that you have all the ability to feel "z" right now. Of course, you shouldn't go through life trying to bliss out with no reason. There, of course, is a median between willfully deciding to be in a good mood and experiencing life events that you find rewarding. If you find yourself in a mood that gives you triggers, you can cause yourself to move out of that mood. You can intentionally will yourself into a better mood by simply focusing your attention on that better mood. Additionally, we can choose to do activities that will encourage us to change our mood. By controlling our internal mind and controlling our activities you will have better control over your mood.

The brain can only focus and give attention to one thought at a time. Despite the claims made by multi-tasking, it is impossible to focus on two things at once. Just as we can focus our attention on something that makes us vulnerable to a trigger, we can similarly shift our focus to something that empowers us. We are more in control of our emotions than we often give ourselves credit. We will go more in-depth over controlling our mood when we talk about the solution to the addiction.

You should note that every slip begins with a trigger, but not every trigger will result in a slip. As you begin the process, you should accept that every trigger will result in a slip. These slips are okay and to be expected. You should not feel bad about slips. Feeling "bad" about slips will very easily result in another immediate trigger that then results in another slip. Instead of focusing on negative emotions, you must learn to change your focus to doing the actions outlined in this book. As you do this, you will eventually get to the point were not every trigger results in a slip. The next step in healing your brain will be a decrease in the number of triggers as well as a reduction in the power of each trigger. Finally, you will reach the point where you no longer experience triggers. At which point your mind has healed itself.

The acronym TROUBLED

There are certain emotions that, when felt, will make you more susceptible to experiencing a trigger and acting out the addiction. [7] The acronym TROUBLED will help you quickly assess your current emotional state. TROUBLED stands for Tired, Regret, Overstressed, Bored, Lonely, Energy, and Depressed. You may find that some emotions are more likely to produce triggers than other emotions. We will talk about creating a journal in the next chapter so that you can see the patterns between certain emotions and their ability to create triggers. Again, these emotions are not bad. They are helpful emotions that are calls to action. Now let's talk about these emotions individually:

Tired

Tired simply means a lack of sleep. If you stay up to study for a test or to finish a research paper, there may be a high probability, for some of you, that you will have a trigger that night or the next day. Again, this is because your Limbic System will over-react to the emotion and interpret it as a threat to survival and then seek refuge with the chemicals provided by the addiction.

Regret

Regret is a feeling we have when we think about our past. Most negative emotions we have that relate to our past could be lumped into regret. As humans, we have a unique ability to remember the past in detail. You do not see this with animals. In the animal world, if geese tussle feathers. You will see them break apart and give each other more space. You won't see one goose holding resentment to another goose. They simply give each other more space and go about their day. If a fish escapes the jaws of an alligator, you will see the fish rejoin the school of fish and go about their day as if nothing happened. You won't see that fish or that school of fish harboring resentment. The school of fish will not try and get revenge on the alligator that tried to eat them. However, with humans, this is different. We will hold resentments towards past experiences and particularly against other people, sometimes for a lifetime. We will often seek and hope for revenge in the future. These feelings we hold for our past are not necessarily bad as a whole, but they should be recognized when felt because they could lead to a trigger.

Overstressed

Where regret relates to our past, stress relates to our fears of the future. If you get a letter from the government saying that they would like to review your tax filing, you are probably going to experience stress over the situation. If your teachers assign excessive amounts of homework or schedule difficult exams, you may feel anxiety. This anxiety of our ability to cope with future events can cause us to be more susceptible to a trigger. Any negative feeling about the future can be lumped into "overstressed."

Uncomfortable

This feeling is kind of a catch-all for any uncomfortable feelings. Something along the lines of "having a bad day." Things just aren't turning out the way you want. Maybe they are not major things. Things like getting caught up in traffic or hitting too many red lights. Or maybe other people are not treating you the way you would want. These things can lead one to feel uncomfortable. Maybe a mild feeling of frustration could be used to describe this category. These subtle yet uncomfortable feelings can cause one to be in a state of mind that would bring on triggers.

Bored

This feeling is what we feel when we want to experience something new, but we do not know what that new experience is, or we feel too tired to do something new. Along with boredom is a feeling of laziness. We probably could find something fun and exciting, but we feel we just don't want to expend the energy to do so. Again, this feeling is probably more unique to the human experience. Boredom can lead you to experience a trigger. Of course, there are better solutions to boredom than addiction.

Lonely

This feeling is probably somewhat self-explanatory. Lonely is feeling a lack of human connection and interaction. If you examine your past triggers and slips, probably most, if not all, have happened when you are alone. You are probably more likely to have a negative emotion (besides lonely) when you are alone versus being in a group.

Energy

This word refers more to our energy level. And more particularly to being hungry or thirsty. Are we out of energy because we need to rest for a moment and eat? Being hungry or thirsty or tired (as mentioned above) can cause us to have a shift in mood that the brain may try to solve through the addiction, thus causing a trigger.

Depressed

If a pet or a loved one dies, we could feel depressed for a time. This feeling is, of course, natural and should not necessarily be avoided. The idea is only to note that you are feeling this way and to see if triggers result from being in this state of mind. This program is not meant as medical advice or meant to diagnose mental problems. If you suffer from severe depression, you will want to seek professional medical help.

Again, the idea of this program is not to avoid these feelings. "Negative" or "Bad" feelings are not necessarily bad for us. They serve a purpose in telling us how we feel, and that action is needed. The problem with someone with an addiction is that they tend to use the addiction to avoid these feelings. The brain will seek refuge in the chemicals produced by the addiction to mask the unwanted feeling. However, this masking only temporarily allows one to escape the emotion. For instance, if you are feeling tired, obviously you need to sleep. However, the addiction may try and solve this feeling of tiredness with the addiction. After feeling the chemicals of the addiction, one might not feel tired for a time, but when those chemicals eventually wear off, you will again be left feeling tired. You may even feel more tired now, which could lead to a Downward Spiral. In a moment, we will talk about the Downward Spiral in more detail. You must start to make the connection between how you feel and your susceptibility to the addiction.

If you have a strong tendency to ignore your emotions, this idea that your emotions trigger your addiction will sound unbelievable. However, it is most likely the case. Later we will talk about writing a journal so you can begin to see how some of these emotions are present when you experience a trigger. Additionally, you will see that some of these emotions are more likely to cause a trigger than others.

Brain Chemicals

Here is a brief list of the brain chemicals that the Limbic System releases and causes the Frontal Lobe to shut down. This list is a shortlist and not comprehensive. However, you will be able to get a good feel for what the Limbic System is trying to accomplish by reviewing this list.

Dopamine:

This chemical is often the first chemical the Limbic System produces and is the chemical that will give us that initial rush of a trigger. This chemical is released before your conscious mind has a chance to respond to information received from your sensory systems. This chemical causes a pleasurable experience that the brain will want to repeat. The brain will experience a heightening of the senses and stimulates memory. This chemical is what causes your heart rate to quicken. [23]

Oxytocin:

This chemical is released after a slip and has a calming effect and is useful in reducing stress. Oxytocin lowers blood pressure and heart rate. [24]

Serotonin:

It also helps create memories, regulates sleep, and creates a feeling of "happiness." It may also help with depression. [25]

Prolactin:

It is associated with the refractory period after sex. It causes relaxation and calming after orgasm. [26]

The brain will release Dopamine first to increase your heart rate and to create excitement and arousal. This chemical is the one that you want to notice when you are trying to observe triggers. This chemical will create a slight uptick in heart rate. The rest of the chemicals, for the most part, happen after orgasm and have the calming effects that the Limbic System seeks to solve all of life's problems.

On the face of it, you may say to yourself that these are good brain chemicals. Why is the addiction causing problems in my life? The problem is that addiction only masks your TROUBLED feelings. These chemicals eventually break down and are consumed. The effects usually only last a few minutes to maybe a few hours. They do not solve the underlying TROUBLED feelings. Illicit drugs also produce desirable moods, feelings, and emotions until they wear off. The same is true with this addiction. Once these mood-enhancing chemicals wear off, you are left with your original problems. You are left with the life events that caused you to feel TROUBLED in the first place. This return to your original TROUBLED state can lead to a repetitive cycle (Downward Spiral).

DeltaFosB:

This chemical deserves to be in a separate category because of its critical role in controlling the Frontal Lobe and creating the addiction. After the other chemicals wear off, not only are you back to your original TROUBLED feeling, but you can also develop another problem, and that is a brain chemical called DeltaFosB.

The brain will begin to produce DeltaFosB, which will cause the brain to lose interest in other lower-level pleasures and seek only the extreme highs caused by the addiction. Once your brain starts experiencing the effects of DeltaFosB, it loses interest in the simpler pleasures of everyday life. This chemical might explain why people with this addiction tend to withdraw from society. They simply lose interest in everyday activities that would only produce mild enjoyment. [27]

Additionally, DeltaFosB does not go away quickly, like the other brain chemicals mentioned above. This chemical lingers in the brain and can last for many weeks. This chemical is what pulls the addicted person back to the addiction even after some time has passed since the last slip. Besides creating new neural pathways, the elimination of DeltaFosB is why this recovery program will take months to complete. It takes time for the brain to cycle through this particular chemical. However, recovery is possible, and this chemical, with time, will leave the brain. The brain was born free from addiction when it was created, and its natural state is to be addiction-free. You just need to give it time to heal. [27]

The Downward Spiral

There is a vicious cycle of addiction that does not let one escape. This vicious cycle can be called the Downward Spiral. This repetitive cycle has everything to do with emotions, which is at the core of triggers. [28] Here is an example of a Downward Spiral:

1. You have a TROUBLED feeling. Let's take tired, for example, the "T" in TROUBLED.
2. Your overactive Limbic System interprets being tired as a threat to survival and desires the brain chemicals produced by the addiction to solve the problem.
3. A slip occurs.

And then the cycle repeats with the possibility of adding additional TROUBLED feelings to the cycle:

1. After the brain chemicals wear off, you are left feeling tired again. Now, not only are you feeling tired, but you feel regret for having had a slip. So now you are feeling the "T" and the "R" in TROUBLED.
2. The overactive Limbic System interprets this as a threat to survival. The Limbic System seeks brain chemicals to solve it.
3. A slip occurs.

Now the Downward Spiral builds even more upon itself:

1. After the brain chemicals wear off, you are left feeling tired and regret. But now you've stayed up a couple of hours past the time you were going to go to bed and realize you will not get enough sleep before you must go to school, and now you feel overstressed. So now you are feeling the "T," the "R" and the "O" of TROUBLED.
2. Your Limbic System interprets an even stronger threat to survival. The Limbic System seeks brain chemicals to solve it.
3. A slip occurs.

The cycle can continue for hours. Each time through a cycle, step 2 is amplified, causing the Limbic System to create an even stronger pull for the calming effects of brain chemicals. The Spiral continues feeding upon itself. This spiral can explain why binges are often associated with addiction. Binging is a natural reaction when you are stuck in the Downward Spiral.

You should note that with the Downward Spiral, you do not necessarily need to add more emotions to keep it going. Only the first emotion is needed. If you do nothing about that emotion, as soon as the brain chemicals wear off, you will be left again with that one negative emotion that will make you susceptible to another slip.

I'm sure you've tried to quit the addiction and were able to abstain from the addiction for a couple of weeks. Eventually, though the addiction catches up, your willpower fails, and you have a slip. You then probably experience a binge because of the extra regret you felt from failing. Binges are signs that an addiction is in effect. [29]

Just quickly, it should be reiterated that during this program, we want to minimize the feelings of regret. If you are actively participating in this program, then regret has served its purpose. Forgiveness should be a priority if you suffer from regret after slips. Try affirmations or meditation to calm this feeling of regret if it is a problem for you. Punishing yourself with regret will not create the desired effect you are seeking. Instead, learn to forgive slips and accept that they will happen as you begin to heal your brain.

The Coolidge Effect

The second main cause for binges besides the Downward Spiral is the Coolidge Effect. The Coolidge Effect is a well-documented phenomenon among most mammals. The phenomenon is that if a male mammal has one sexual partner, the male will reach "sexual satiation" quickly. Sexual satiation is the idea that after sex, there is little desire to have another sexual experience. This reduction in desire is called the "refractory period" after sex, where a male is physically/mentally unable to have another sexual experience.

Just briefly here is the story about how the Coolidge Effect got its name:

There is an amusing story about the American president, Calvin Coolidge, who once visited a farm with his wife. Soon after their arrival, they were taken off on separate tours. When Mrs. Coolidge passed the chicken pens, she paused to ask the man in charge if the rooster copulates

more than once each day. "Dozens of times," was the reply. "Please tell that to the President," Mrs. Coolidge requested. When the President passed the pens and was told about the rooster, he asked: "Same hen every time?" "Oh no, Mr. President, a different one each time." The President nodded slowly, then said, "Tell that to Mrs. Coolidge." In light of this story, the expression "The Coolidge Effect" was coined for the phenomenon of male re-arousal by a new female. The Coolidge effect is widespread among mammals.
- A. Ben-Zeév Ph.D., "In the Name of Love" [30]

This humorous story about the United States President Calvin Coolidge illustrates perfectly how the Coolidge Effect affects males with a high number of sexually willing females (novel females). The male will not reach sexual satiation, and the refractory period will be reduced. The male will have the ability and desire to mate many more times than if the male had a limited number of sexual partners. [31]

If you are suffering from binges, there is an extremely high probability that your brain is experiencing the Coolidge Effect. Some signs that you have suffered from the Coolidge Effect include:

- Having multiple slips in a short span of a couple of hours by watching different adult performers or different genres of adult material
- Maintaining sexual desire or an erection longer than you are able during traditional lovemaking
- Finding the "perfect" adult performer in your estimations only to quickly lose interest and move on to other adult performers
- Choosing the addiction over lovemaking
- Thinking about adult material to maintain an erection or to achieve orgasm during lovemaking

Just like being able to define an emotion helps neutralize the effects of that emotion, being able to define the Coolidge Effect helps neutralize its power over you. You know what is happening and why it is happening simply by calling it the Coolidge Effect. It shows you that you are not alone and that others have a similar reaction as you do. You also begin to understand the game that is being played in your mind.

Think about games that involve strategy. For example, American Football; if you see your opponent is going to "blitz," then you can prepare for the quarterback to throw the football quickly if it's a pass play. If you're playing chess and you see your opponent is using the "Queen's Gambit" against you, just by naming the strategy of your opponent allows you to defend yourself better and make counter moves. This ability to name the Coolidge Effect really is beneficial in our fight against the addiction. Naming the action allows you to take the surprise out of that action and gives you confidence because not only are you aware of what is happening, but you will already have a counter plan. The ability to give a name to what is happening is part of the idea that if you know yourself and you know your enemy, you will inevitably win (Sun Tzu).

By naming the Coolidge Effect, you will be able to prepare yourself and take action to limit its effect.

Do not hate the Coolidge Effect, but be thankful for it. When our distant ancestors were up against the elements, there were times when a large percentage of the men did not come back home from hunting. They may have been slaughtered by another group of animals or were unprepared for changes in weather. This wiring helped the surviving men create the next generation when few men were left. Also, it allowed for harmony as well. When the ratio of men and women were in balance, men did not go insane with trying to mate with every female. There was sexual satiation within the men. Modern society's sexual satiation is something that is still important. It allows the male to have the ability to have long term pair bonding. It allows a man to be able to have the traditional idea of "a wife and kids." The desire to be with other women can be inhibited by reaching sexual satiation with a single woman.

The Brain Was Not Meant for Continuous Chemical Releases

The brain was born without addiction, and the brain's natural state is to be addiction free. The brain desires to be in its natural state. The brain will begin to try and minimize the effects of this continuous rush of powerful brain chemicals to return to a non-addicted state. The brain does this by shutting off some of the brain receptors for pleasure. Shutting off brain receptors is the brain's attempt to allow the brain to return to normal. [15]

However, an overactive Limbic System will remain unaffected and will continue to seek brain chemicals to solve all of life's problems. As stated, the Limbic System thinks it has found the Holy Grail, the solution to all of life's problems. It believes it has found a panacea. It will continue to seek the addiction despite the brain's attempt to turn off receptors.

In response to the shutting down of brain receptors, the Limbic system will either seek out a higher high or saturate the brain for a longer period with brain chemicals.

Create a Higher High

The Limbic System may seek out a higher high to maximize the use of remaining brain receptors. This strategy causes the addicted person to be tempted to watch more graphic images than he would otherwise view, thereby connecting different areas of the brain that normally are not active during sex. The Limbic System attempts to create a more heightened experience. So, images that are shocking or emotionally charged, such as violent or illegal adult material, will activate parts of the brain that are not normally activated during a sexual experience. Combining different areas of the brain allows the Limbic System to deliver brain chemicals to new areas of the brain. Thereby heighten the high of a slip despite the brain shutting down pleasure receptors located in parts of the brain that would normally be active during a sexual experience. In extreme cases, some people with the addiction have even seen their viewing change to images that do not match their sexual orientation to achieve this new high. [32]

Saturation

A sign of addiction is the amount of influence the activity has on a person's life. Certainly, the length of time spent on addiction would be a sign of severe addiction. [33] If the Limbic System tries to saturate the brain, then it will try to view adult images for an extended period. If you've ever watched adult material for hours on end, then your Limbic System is trying to saturate your brain. The Limbic System is trying to exploit the pleasure receptors that are still functioning to the highest degree possible. The Limbic System will exploit the Downward Spiral and the Coolidge Effect to release brain chemicals for a length of time that is unnatural compared to normal lovemaking. Normal sexual experiences usually last minutes and usually less than an hour. However, an overactive Limbic System may try and saturate the brain by watching graphic images for multiple hours.

Whether the overactive Limbic System seeks more graphic material or lengthening the time interval, it shows us that the addiction is not based on sexual desire but instead based on a desire for brain chemicals. Having consistent sexual experiences is not a solution to this addiction. It is not based on our desire for sex but instead, brain chemicals. If it were based on merely our desire to have sex, then it would not seek out ever more graphic imagery, and it would not seek out ever longer periods. You need to make this distinction between sex (natural lovemaking or wet dreams) and brain chemicals. While the Limbic System does hijack the circuitry used for rewarding sex, it does this to release brain chemicals. The problem is not your desire for sex, which is natural and good when used appropriately; the problem is your desire for brain chemicals.

After you overcome this addiction, your brain will still desire sex and to find a sexual partner. However, it will no longer have the unnatural desire to cure all of life's problems with brain chemicals. This concept is an important distinction that you need to understand. Your sexual desire is completely different than your desire for brain chemicals. Sexual desire is natural, while brain chemicals are unnatural. Your problem is brain chemicals and not the desire for sex.

Teenagers and Addiction

Teenagers start their addiction at the peak of their neuroplasticity and dopamine levels. While the brain reaches, for the most part, its full size around age 6 there is a reorganization of the brain that will happen between the ages of 12 and 25. A person will experience a radical change in the structure of their brain. This restructuring allows the brain to process information at a faster rate but makes it difficult to learn new skills. To create a quicker brain, some pathways that have not been used will be removed from the brain. Once the brain has reorganized and becomes faster, it becomes harder for neuroplasticity to occur (the ability to create new neural pathways and learn new skills). The saying "you can't teach a dog new tricks" illustrates this point. [12]

Teenagers tend to be sensation seeking. It is not that teens underestimate risks but that teens put an over-emphasis on rewards. For teens, this desire for rewards, the benefits of an action, creates a stronger desire for brain chemicals, and negates the negative consequences of the addiction. [12]

Not only are the rewards given priority against negative consequences, but at no other time in a person's life do brain chemicals last as long. Brain chemicals last longer in the teenage brain, giving them the most heightened experiences from the addiction. [34]

Here are some startling statistics:

- 90% of Americans who meet the medical criteria for addiction started smoking, drinking or using other drugs before age 18 [1]
- 1 in 4 Americans who began using any addictive substance before age 18 are addicted, compared to 1 in 25 who started using at age 21 or older [1]

So here are some inferences that can be made. If you are between the ages of 12 and 25, time is of the essence. This period is your best chance at quick brain changes. You may still be at your best neuroplasticity. Creating new neural pathways may come easier for you, so take advantage of this time. Focus on the rewards of being addiction free such as gaining self-confidence and increased creativity. Focus on rewards more than consequences because this plays to the natural abilities of your brain.

If you are over the age of 25, your recovery may take longer to achieve, but brain plasticity is still a reality. An example of the brain's ability to change has been done with experiments with inversion goggles/glasses. Subjects were given goggles that inverted the image so that the subject saw the world upside down. Subjects wore these goggles for around 5 to 8 days, and the brain was able to correct for the goggles and created the world right-side-up again. When the goggles were removed, and the subjects used their normal vision, the world again appeared upside down even though the goggles had been removed. The brain was able to reestablish the original neural pathways in about an hour and not the 5 to 8 days it took to create a brand new neural pathway. This experiment was also done using inversion from side to side. This experiment took 2 months for the brain to switch the images, but again, once the goggles were removed, it only took a few hours for the brain to reestablish the original neural pathway and to see the world as normal. The subjects were adults. If you are over 25 the brain can create new neural pathways. It might take some time, but it can happen. [35]

Also, the more years of life you lived before becoming addicted will help your mind reestablish prior neural pathways that functioned before the addiction began. If you created the addiction early in your teen years, it might be harder to reestablish the original, non-addicted pathways than someone who started the addiction later in their teen years.

These are all just estimates. Everyone creates neural pathways at a different rate. What is crucial in creating neural pathways is consistency. In the goggle experiments, it might have been impossible for the subjects to create a new neural pathway if the subjects wore the goggles one day and took them off the next. Keep consistency in mind as you go through this program. Consistency is critical. Once you start the program, do not stop till you have achieved the desired result.

No "Rock Bottom" for this Addiction

When compared to other addictions, a person with an addiction to adult material is often considered "high functioning." Meaning that they can keep a job or stay in school. [36] If you look at someone addicted to alcohol or drugs, the brain will crave more and more alcohol or drugs to get to that previous high. Each time the brain and body are trying to resist the drugs. The brain begins to shut down the receptors for pleasure that are associated with taking the drug. The addicted person is then forced to take a higher dose of the drug to reach a similar high. Eventually, there is a point where the body cannot physically take on more drug consumption. With some drugs, there is a point of overdose where the body stops functioning, and the person dies. With other drugs, the body loses certain organ and bodily functions, and it becomes painfully clear that the person needs help.

Unlike a substance addiction, for us, there is no "rock bottom." The person will often be able to mask the bad effects of this addiction from others. Eventually, people may think that the addicted person is just a negative or moody person. They may think that the person has low social desires or has bad people skills. Sexual partners may even think that the person has a low libido, which may not be the case. Given enough time, people around the addicted person will just accept the change.

For you, there is no physical rock bottom where the body will break down. However, there is something just as devastating, and that is the years that can go by before you begin your recovery. Many of us became addicted during our teen years due to how the teenage brain is wired. So, the lack of a rock bottom can be devastating for those of us that began in the teenage years. Essentially, we never knew what it meant to have an adult life without addiction. As a result, many of us will consider this addiction as something normal. Many of us may accept viewing adult material as something that adults do. Essentially never knowing the captivity that addiction has on our life. Essentially living a lie and not even knowing it, living as a captive, and not even knowing it.

For some, the realization of captivity comes due to some inability to perform sexually. Whether from erectile dysfunction or the inability to have an orgasm without the use of visualizing adult material. For many, it is at that point that the evidence of captivity to the addiction cannot be ignored.

For others, the realization of captivity comes from a loved one. If we can humble ourselves enough, we will see the truth about what they tell us. It is incredibly hard for someone to be told they have a problem. We need to look at the other person's intention and realize they are trying to help more than criticize.

For some, the realization of captivity comes from religion. It is probably safe to say that most religions either completely forbid adult material or discourage the viewing of it. For religious purposes, someone may try to quit the addiction. After many failed attempts at quitting, the person may realize that addiction has formed.

It is important to note that hitting rock bottom is not necessary for recovery. Simply the realization that addiction has formed and the desire to stop is what is needed. Desire is the number one determinant.

The Brain's Ability for Rapid Imagery

For most of us, our strategy to quit the addiction was to clench our fist and tell ourselves to "stop watching pornography" or a similar variation of that phrase. Of course, the instant we say the word "pornography," our mind begins to go to work. It will start to bring up imagery that is associated with that word. Of course, that is the opposite of what we want.

The brain is incredibly fast, especially when it comes to interpreting images. A study at MIT found that the brain can process images as fast as 13 milliseconds. [37] While the speed of the brain is usually an advantage, we must be aware of this speed and not try and ignore that our brains are often faster than we consciously understand.

To further explain the idea, I will tell you to not think about something. Do not think about a #2 lead pencil.

Even though I told you not to think about a #2 lead pencil, you probably imagined a yellow pencil with an aluminum metal band that attaches a red eraser to the end of the pencil. Maybe you went a step further to imagine doing math or filling out a bubble sheet with a pencil. After reading these sentences, it is guaranteed that you imagined in your mind a pencil. Now do not imagine that pencil turning from yellow to purple. Even though you're not supposed to imagine a pencil or even a purple pencil, your brain probably had no problem imagining a purple #2 pencil even if you have never seen a purple pencil in real life.

What we resist persists.

-C.G. Jung (Swiss psychiatrist)

Telling the brain to not think about something is a losing man's battle. Resisting the addiction by focusing on how much we want to stop is only causing the brain to focus on the addition making the addiction stronger. Instead, we must work with the brain and give it something else to focus on instead of the addiction. By resisting the addiction, you are actually telling your mind to focus on it. By resisting the addiction, you make the addiction the most prominent idea in your mind. You can see why resisting the addiction is a waste of time. We must shift our focus to healing an overactive Limbic System instead of trying to use willpower to resist triggers. By focusing on healing the brain from undesirable brain chemicals, only then can we make the addiction beatable.

To win the war, we must make a huge paradigm switch in the way we view our addition. We cannot resist pornography and win the war. Pornography has zero importance to recover. We need to focus our efforts on training our brains not to crave brain chemicals. This change in focus is an extremely important concept to understand. If we are to win the war, we must know who the true enemy is. And that enemy is not adult material but an overactive

Limbic System of the brain. We must work with the brain and how it functions if we are going to be able to create lasting change. So instead of telling your brain to not think about something, instead start asking your brain why it is seeking brain chemicals. What emotion is the addiction trying to escape? You must make this paradigm switch and shift your focus to overcoming this addiction.

Learn to become still and to take your attention away from what you don't want, and all the emotional charge around it, and place the attention on what you wish to experience.

- Michael Beckwith (Motivation speaker - author)

Steps to Create Lasting Change

From Tony Robbins, to create lasting change, there is a simple three-step process: desire, a role model, and overcome internal contradicting beliefs.

Step 1: The first step to creating lasting change is to have commitment and desire. You need to know what you want and why you want it. Desire will keep you going even after there are obstacles that need to be overcome. We covered this in the introduction.

Step 2: You need a coach or a role model. You need someone who has already achieved what you want to accomplish. They can tell you how to do it and pitfalls to avoid. The RAMP program is your coach so that you understand how the game is being played in your mind, and then you will have strategies and activities to allow your brain to heal. A coach is also important for consistency. If you need more interaction and support, join the Reddit group NoFap at http://www.reddit.com/r/NoFap/

Step 3: You need to overcome internal contradicting beliefs. These contradicting beliefs go along the lines of excuses. Sometimes we know we are using excuses to take the responsibility away from ourselves. However, sometimes, these excuses go a step beyond and turn in to actual beliefs that we have developed. Beliefs that we think are true, even though they are not.

These contradicting beliefs can be attached to triggers. Basically, during your recovery, you will find some triggers that are not only based on emotion but additionally have a belief surrounding them as to why the trigger is justifiable. You will discover that these beliefs are tied to specific triggers. These triggers need special attention. For me, I had two beliefs that I had to overcome that were tied to triggers. The first was feeling tired. I had the belief that I needed the calming brain chemicals for me to sleep. It was more than just feeling tired; there was a belief behind the trigger as well. It seems simple enough, but this was one of my last triggers to overcome during my recovery. I solved it by creating a routine sleep cycle and by using sleep aids to establish my sleep pattern. Another belief that I had was that I was justified in my addiction if my wife did not want to have intercourse. This belief was tied to the triggers of loneliness and regret. I needed to change my belief so that I felt I was never justified in acting out on the addiction. Again, this sounds simple enough, but this was one of the last triggers to linger before recovery was achieved.

You may discover the same during your recovery, that certain triggers are harder to overcome than others. Be aware that there may be a belief that needs to be overcome in addition to doing RAMP and doing your modifying activity for that emotion.

To help overcome contradicting beliefs, you can use mental rehearsals and affirmations to access the subconscious mind to overcome these beliefs. We will discuss these two activities in the next chapter.

Key Takeaways from Chapter 2

1. The Triple-A Engine of the internet is availability, anonymity, and affordability. The internet allows people who otherwise would not develop an addiction to develop one, including under-aged people.

2. The Limbic System of the brain is the cause of addiction. However, your Frontal Lobe is the part of your brain that can heal the Limbic System.

3. The acronym TROUBLED stands for Tired, Regret, Overstressed, Uncomfortable, Bored, Lonely, Energy, and Depressed. These emotions trigger a survival response in the overactive Limbic System.

4. Brain chemicals involved in the addiction include, but not limited to, Dopamine, Oxytocin, Serotonin, and DeltaFosB chemicals.

5. The Downward Spiral of the addiction causes one to have multiple slips, often creating more TROUBLED emotions that stack up on top of themselves. Binges are a sign of addiction.

6. The Coolidge Effect shortens the Refractory Period and allows a male to have multiple slips with the introduction of a novel female. Like the Downward Spiral, the Coolidge Effect allows one to binge on the addiction.

7. The brain was not meant for continuous chemical releases and will shut off pleasure receptors in the brain. The Limbic System will then try to heighten the addiction with more graphic images or through saturation by extending the length of time viewing.

8. The teenage brain puts a greater emphasis on reward than on risk. It is much easier to develop an addiction in the teenage years than any other stage of life. This addiction often carries on through adulthood.

9. Triggers begin the moment that the Limbic System releases chemicals, creating an overwhelming urge for the addiction. Triggers are made up of a reminder of sex and an emotional state.

10. The addiction allows one to remain high functioning, thereby creating no rock bottom for the addicted person. A rock bottom is not necessary for recovery, only a desire for recovery.

11. The brain was built to process information rapidly. It is impossible to tell your brain to not think about something. You will be more effective in giving the brain a new focus.

Chapter 3: The RAMP Solution

Before describing RAMP, you need to know three important rules to the RAMP solution. And they are:

- RULE 1: Once RAMP has started it does not stop until each letter is completed.
- RULE 2: Once RAMP has started it does not stop until each letter is completed.
- RULE 3: Once RAMP has started it does not stop until each letter is completed.

If I can steal the real estate agent's moto of the three most important things about real estate (location, location, and location), the three most important things about this program are completing RAMP consistently with every trigger. I cannot tell you how important consistency is in this solution. I haven't even told you what the acronym RAMP stands for because the first three rules are that important to the solution. Do you remember the upside-down goggle experiment? Not completing RAMP would be like one of the test subjects taking off the goggles for a day. There is nothing more damaging to your progress than skipping an opportunity to complete RAMP. NOTHING!

Consistency is extremely important. For example, if you ask yourself consistently, every day, when did you put your shoes on? Even though the event of putting on your shoes is, for the most part, mundane and unimportant. You better believe your brain is going to make that moment of your day memorable. It doesn't know why you ask the question if it is a matter of life or death; it only knows that it is going to be asked, and that consistency of asking every day is what makes it important. The brain changes because of consistency. Recovery means healing your brain. In that process, you are literally changing the shape of your brain. Recovery truly is mind over matter. If you are going to change the shape of your brain, then you must have consistency. The cliché "practice makes perfect" is speaking directly about consistency.

Additionally, these brain chemicals will tempt you to believe that everything is fine and that the addiction has cured your TROUBLED state. We know that to be a lie. We need consistency to show the Limbic System an alternative to the addiction. Nothing in this world is more precious to the Limbic System than this addiction. As stated above, it thinks it has found the Holy Grail, the cure-all to life's problems. We must offer the Limbic System an alternative to this Holy Grail. The alternative may not be as good as the addiction, but with time the Limbic System will accept the alternative as good enough. Also, you will be strengthening the Frontal Lobe, which in turn will demand that the Limbic System accept the alternative.

Once RAMP has started, it does not stop until each letter is completed!

There is no other way around this rule. There are no excuses. The completion of all steps must happen consistently. So, without further ado, I give you the RAMP solution:

RAMP – Recognize, Action, Modify and Praise (Party)

Recognize

The first step is to Recognize. Recognize the moment you have a trigger. Remember, a trigger can be broken down into two parts. A reminder of sex and your emotional state when you have that reminder. The Limbic System gets first dibs on your sensory systems. The Limbic System will automatically release brain chemicals in anticipation of a slip. That release of chemicals can be felt in the body. The biggest tell that chemicals have been released is a slight uptick in your heart rate caused by dopamine.

This release of dopamine can happen way before the viewing of adult material. Only the thought that eventually a slip will occur is all that is necessary to have a trigger. You might be sitting in a classroom and the realization that later in the day, you will be home alone. That realization can cause a trigger while in the classroom. The emotional state that is felt is one of loneliness, the "L" in TROUBLED, the reminder of sex is caused internally by your memory. So even though you might be hours away from being home alone, a trigger has happened.

Now, when you first begin the program, these triggers may be elusive. You might not be able to tell exactly when a trigger happens, but with practice, you will become more sensitive. When you create your journal entry, you will ask yourself, "When did the trigger happen?" and your brain will begin to search for the answer. As you consistently ask yourself this question, after each trigger, your subconscious mind will begin to monitor your body throughout the day, and it will begin to detect triggers the moment they happen. The subconscious mind will begin to recognize the event. The subconscious mind will then alert the conscious mind that a trigger is happening. Again, consistency is paramount in creating this detection system within your brain.

If you doubt this process, there is an exercise you can do that will prove the subconscious mind's ability to monitor events. You can follow this process with dreams. Ask yourself to remember your dream just as you are falling asleep. Then when you wake up, even before you get out of bed or even open your eyes, think about your dreams and try to remember them. Next, write them down with a pen and paper. You will notice after a week or two that your dreams become more vivid and more real and that your ability to remember dreams has significantly increased. Now your conscious mind is asleep. It is not aware of the dream, but your subconscious mind is still active. Your subconscious mind knows it needs to remember this dream because it's going to be asked to remember the event. It does this with no active effort on your part. It has been trained through consistency that it needs to remember dreams. So it does. The subconscious mind is very powerful. To access this power, we need to use consistency. Consistency is the key.

Eventually, you will get to the point that you can detect the very instance a trigger happens. You can then significantly limit the quantity of brain chemicals released by the Limbic System by following the next steps of RAMP. Limiting the quantity of chemicals released will give you the best chance to avoiding a slip. If you can reduce the quantity of brain chemicals in the brain, your Frontal Lobe has a better chance of staying active and functional, allowing you the conscious choice to not go through with the addiction.

Action

As the addiction needs a reminder of sex, in your solution, you will create a reminder to follow through with RAMP. This reminder is done by touching the thumb against another finger. You can pick any finger you want with whichever thumb. The main idea is that it is always that same thumb with that same finger. This action shows the body that you are in control of physical movements and that you are consciously alert to the fact that a trigger has happened.

Next, you need to shift your body position to an alert state. When you are in a TROUBLED state, it is almost certain that your body is not in a position of alertness and power. Your shoulders are probably hunched over, and your head is down. You want to reposition your body into that of strength. Straighten your spinal column. Stand up straight if you are standing or sit up straight if you are sitting. Get your shoulders back and your head up. Simply changing your body position will lessen the power of the TROUBLED emotional state.

Next, you need to take deep breaths. These deep breaths should last about one minute. You don't need to draw attention to yourself, and you don't need to hyperventilate, but you do need to make a conscious effort to expand your lungs during each breath fully. Momentarily hold the air just slightly longer than a normal breath then exhale. As you take these dozen or so deep breaths, consciously feel the air move into your lungs and back out. This process alone will tell your body that you are not in a life or death situation. The overactive Limbic System likes to overdramatize a TROUBLED state into a life and death situation. Breathing deep and consciously, focusing on your breaths tells your body this is not the case. There is no threat to life.

Breathing deeply also increases oxygen in the blood. Your body needs oxygen; however, the Frontal Lobe is probably the most sensitive to oxygen. If your body is unable to receive oxygen, one of the greatest risks is brain damage. More particularly, damage to the Frontal Lobe. The Limbic System and the other organs in your body will most likely start functioning perfectly again if oxygen is restored to the blood promptly. However, it only takes minutes for the Frontal Lobe to suffer serious damage from a lack of oxygen. That is how important oxygen is to the Frontal Lobe. It functions best with oxygenated blood. Breathing deep kicks your Frontal Lobe into high gear. It allows the Frontal Lobe to stay functioning despite the brain chemicals of the Limbic System.

Now, as you start this program, you are most likely going to give in to the addiction and give into the brain chemicals it produces. You are most likely going to have a slip while in the RAMP process. That is ok. That is perfectly fine. The idea is to keep your Frontal Lobe functioning as long as possible so that it can note the two parts of the trigger for your journal entry.

The Frontal Lobe can begin to analyze the trigger and find a better solution than what the addiction can provide. It can find a real solution to your TROUBLED state. Get as far as you can in the RAMP process before the slip occurs. It's okay that you have a slip, but the idea is to keep progressing along with RAMP. After a slip and the brain chemicals wear off, your Frontal Lobe will come back online. You then need to proceed where you left off with the RAMP process and complete the rest of the steps. Nothing should stop you from completing RAMP, and that includes slips. It does not matter if a slip occurs or not; you will complete RAMP. If a trigger happens, RAMP begins. Slips are no longer a focus or a concern to you. Finishing RAMP is your main concern. Remember, what we resist persists. We are shifting our focus away from slips, and we are now focusing on completing the RAMP process.

With time and consistency, your Frontal Lobes will become more resistant to brain chemicals as you force your Frontal Lobes to function longer and longer after a trigger occurs. Do not feel discouraged in the beginning that you are not able to resist brain chemicals and have slips while completing RAMP. Be confident that with some time, you will improve to the point where you can get through RAMP without having a slip. Allow yourself time to heal. You are creating new neural pathways, and this takes time.

The faster you become at recognizing a trigger, the sooner you can start your "action." If you catch yourself fast enough, there is a good chance that your "action" will be able to calm the Limbic System down. You'll be able to limit the amount of brain chemicals released. Even though the power of the trigger has been dissipated and you no longer feel the need to have a slip, you still need to complete RAMP. Again, once RAMP has started, it does not stop until each letter is completed! There are no excuses, even if you think the trigger has been removed. You complete RAMP all the way through.

Remember the rules: Once RAMP has started, it does not stop until each letter is completed.

Modify

Triggers are tied to emotions. You need to be able to create a "modifying activity" to put you in a better state. Often the modifying activity that you need is obvious. For example, if you are feeling tired, the "T" in TROUBLED, simply taking a power nap may be sufficient. If you are feeling lonely, then connecting with someone face to face would be an appropriate modifying activity. Even connecting via text or social media may suffice. Even though you're modifying activity (modifying behavior) may not seem complicated, it cannot be overlooked. You must be able to change your state of mind without the use of the addiction.

Remember, when we talked about emotion in chapter 1. Emotions follow a process, and part of that process is a stimulus (either external or internal). We then pass judgment on that stimulus to create an emotion. Modifying activities focus on creating positive external stimuli to give us reasons to have positive emotions. By doing a beneficial activity, a modifying activity, you will give yourself an external stimulus to feel positive emotions. Positive emotions will tell your Limbic System that it does not need to be overstimulated that there is no threat to life and to relax. With time, the Limbic System will accept modifying activities as sufficient solutions to TROUBLED emotions.

As a warning, you need to recognize that slips have a false calming effect. If you have a slip, at that moment, you may feel fine and that you no longer have a trigger. However, you still need to go through with your modifying activity. You must be able to tell your Limbic System that there is a better solution to your TROUBLED state than the addiction. The Limbic System will not accept your modifying activity as being equal to the addiction, but, with time, it will accept the modifying activity as being good enough.

Remember, consistency is paramount. We want to consistently show the Limbic System that there is a solution for TROUBLED feelings outside of the addiction. We need to consistently show that being bored, the "B" in TROUBLED, is not a life and death situation and that there are other solutions to boredom that do not consist of acting out the addiction. Consistency is extremely important.

Also, at every opportunity, you will want to take full advantage of exercise. Exercise is incredibly important and should be considered the atomic bomb in your fight against the Limbic System. There may be times when you are unsure which TROUBLED feeling is behind the trigger. If this is the case, make an educated guess to the TROUBLED feeling and do your modifying activity, but along with the modifying activity, include a visit to the gym. Also consider that exercise can be a modifying activity in and of itself. It could be a solution to regret, overstress, uncomfortable, and depressed emotions.

After your modifying activity, really allow yourself to feel good, which brings us to our last step in RAMP.

Praise (Party)

Praise may sound like the least important step, but it holds a critical key in your recovery. This important step is to praise yourself for completing RAMP. Praise yourself for going through with the modifying activity. Too many people are unwilling to make the sacrifice, to actually do something about their addiction. They're more willing to use excuses for the addiction. As mentioned above, they use excuses such as everyone is addicted, it doesn't affect me, or it is impossible to quit. They are liars and wimps. However, you are fighting the good fight. You are better than this addiction. You're willing to put in the effort, burn off the DeltaFosB chemicals, and create new neural pathways.

You need to give yourself pause and congratulate yourself on completing RAMP. Give yourself pause to allow yourself to really feel the effects of the modifying activity. Allow yourself to focus on positive emotions. These positive emotions will allow you to go a longer period before experiencing another trigger. If you had a slip during your progression through RAMP, this moment of praising yourself will limit the addiction's ability to create a Downward Spiral. You must focus on the positive emotions felt from your modifying activity and from exercising. And it also trains your Limbic System to accept the modifying activity as a satisfactory replacement for the addiction.

Again, emotions come from stimulus, both external and internal, that we then judge to create an emotion. Whereas modifying activities focus on external stimulus to create emotion, self-praise focuses on internal stimulus to create positive emotions. When you can do activities that create uplifting emotions through manipulating external and internal stimuli, eventually, your Limbic System will stop being overactive and will allow you to cure your TROUBLED emotion with the RAMP process instead of the addiction. Praise is the last step in creating a positive internal stimulus for an uplifting change in mood.

Perhaps the best way to create this positive vibe is to share it with someone else. You don't have to share your RAMP experience with someone else completely, but you'll be perfectly fine sharing your new positive mood with someone else. If you're able to share your positive emotion with someone else, it allows you to experience the positive emotion anew. Connecting with someone else with your positive emotion allows you to double its effect. Don't discount human interaction. It is incredibly helpful in uplifting you and allowing you to relive your positive experience after your modifying activity. Connecting with someone else is the "Party" part of the RAMP solution. To party, you need to have other people share your enjoyment. This sharing does not need to be complex. Sending out a cheerful text message or a message on a social media website is all that is needed.

The "P" in RAMP is designed to work with who you are. There are two aspects to the "P," which are Praise and Party. If you are an introvert, you will probably find the internal Praise comes naturally to you. And if you are an extrovert, you will probably find the external Party comes naturally to you. Do what works for you, but also push yourself to do both the internal Praise and the external Party of RAMP. You benefit from doing both aspects of "P" whether you are an introvert or an extrovert.

Even if you had a slip during the process of RAMP, do not let a slip cause you from being able to enjoy your modifying activity. You may feel regret for having slipped, but it does you no good to focus on this emotion. This time of praise/party is a time to train your Limbic System in releasing healthy levels of brain chemicals. It teaches the Limbic System that enjoyment can be felt from simpler everyday activities.

The focus on praising yourself is designed to limit the negative self-talk someone with an addiction may have. This focus on self-praise allows you to have a defined win during your recovery, even if you had a slip. Winning gives you a sense of accomplishment and the motivation to continue and have more wins. With time, your brain will heal, and when you have a TROUBLED feeling, your Limbic System's first reaction will not be to seek out the addiction. Instead, the Limbic System will want the modifying activity and the rewards that come with it.

Finding Modifying Activities

It should be noted that since you have a brain that is wired for addiction that you could develop an addiction to other substances. Do not pick modifying activities that could lead to other addictions. So, you wouldn't want to choose an activity that deals with alcohol or drugs. That would only cause you to replace one addiction for another. Instead, choose modifying activities that will uplift you emotionally.

As a warning, behavioral addictions, such as this one, tend to react in the brain as a stimulant. Avoid any drug that would be classified as a stimulant. [2]

The goal of modifying activities is to emotionally engage you in an activity that is more healthy and beneficial to you than the addiction. These modifying activities should be used to satisfy the TROUBLED emotion that is associated with your trigger.

If you have been addicted for many years, you may have forgotten what hobbies you liked before the addiction. A good activity will be to explore your childhood. What did you do in your childhood that you could do for hours? There were emotions in these activities that attracted you to them, and there is a good chance that similar activities will still be attractive to you today. Maybe you liked fishing. Maybe you liked riding your bike. Maybe you liked camping. Maybe you liked board games. These activities have their equivalent in the adult world.

For instance, if you enjoyed riding your bicycle. Ask yourself what was it about riding a bicycle that fascinated you. Was it the feeling of exploration or the exhilaration of air rushing over you? If it was being in the open air, you could try mountain biking or riding a motorcycle as your modifying activity. If you liked exploring new places, you could begin setting up a vacation in a part of the world you have never been to as your modifying activity. You could also consider learning a second language to facilitate your new modifying activity to travel abroad. It's not hard to see how these activities could effectively be used to combat TROUBLED feelings.

Another example is if you liked fishing as a kid. Now, as an adult, you could make a goal to catch every species of game fish in the area that you live. This modifying activity would not only include the fishing trip but the planning as well. Go on the internet and learn the different techniques used to catch each species of fish. Plan out where you will stay when visiting a lake, ocean, or river. Will you be camping, staying at a hotel or making a day trip? All this planning and preparation would be a great modifying activity to combat TROUBLED feelings. Certainly, planning a trip would cause a shift in attitude if one was feeling bored or overstressed. In addition to planning the trip, you could find other people who enjoy your hobby and reach out to them for tips on fishing. Reaching out to others could combat a feeling of loneliness. There are plenty of online communities that are dedicated to your modifying activity.

There are many different hobbies you can find that would interest you. Thinking back to your childhood will allow you to find some possible modifying activities quickly. Hobbies are an essential part of creating modifying activities. Think of these hobbies as rewards for your dedication to quitting the addiction.

Some people may think you are rewarding yourself because of the addiction, but this is not the case. You may need to explain that the addiction, in many ways, has isolated you from the rest of the world. A way to combat the addiction is to break this isolation and to have life experiences that allow you to feel a healthy release of brain chemicals. The solution to the addiction lies in finding healthy outlets for your TROUBLED feelings. You are not rewarding bad behavior but discovering new outlets to create a better life. You are rewarding a new way to live life. Also, remember this addiction feeds off negative emotions, so punishments will not create the emotions needed to combat this addiction. Instead, focus on rewards to create emotions that will combat this addiction.

You must be able to find modifying activities that the Limbic System will accept as good enough. No modifying activity will match the chemical release of the addiction. However, with time, you can find modifying activities that release just enough pleasurable chemicals that the Limbic System will have no other choice but to believe that a threat to survival is not happening. This shift will only happen with consistency. Even if you have a slip you still need to go through with your modifying activity even if the chemical release of the addiction has happened. <u>Once RAMP starts, it does not stop until it has been fully completed.</u>

You may even feel fine after a slip but, again, this is a lie. The events that caused the underlying emotion associated with the trigger/slip have not changed. You must do the actions necessary to change your emotional state, which is done by doing your modifying activity and the other activities of RAMP. With consistency, the Limbic System will recognize that there are other activities, other modifying activities, which can create a satisfactory condition where the rush of chemicals of the addiction is unnecessary.

Make a list of these modifying activities and put them in your journal after the "Letter from Future Self," which we will now talk about creating.

Letter from Future Self

To start your journal, we'll write a letter from your future self to your present self. Doing this will allow you to connect the benefits of overcoming the addiction that you will realize in your future to your present. Sometimes it is hard to focus on or believe in the benefits that will happen in the future. So, to do this, we will write a letter from who you are without the addiction to your present-day self.

In the book *The Willpower Instinct: How Self-Control Works, Why It Matters, and What You Can Do to Get More of It* by Kelly McGonigal Ph.D., she talks about Self-Defining Future Memory. It is the idea that not only can we use past experiences to define who we are, but we can also create vivid images of our future to do the same. This future memory could reflect new values of what we will become. By creating a future memory, we connect who we will be in the future to who we are today. This connection with the future gives us greater determination to make changes today so that we can realize the future memory. We can do this by writing a letter to ourselves about this self-defining future memory.

Your future memory should be something that creates positive emotions within you. Maybe it would be a feeling of quiet satisfaction and being at peace with yourself. Perhaps it involves a loved one (wife, daughter, or son). It is easy to create emotions around someone you have or will have a powerful personal connection. Create this memory in your mind. This future self should be 10 or 20 years into your future. So, if you don't have a wife, daughter, or son yet, but you could imagine your future self of 10 to 20 years having these loved ones in your future life, then have them in your future memory. Maybe you don't know what they will look like, so instead, just imagine their voice.

For instance, you could create a vivid memory such as this example: It's a Saturday morning, and you have the day off. You are pouring yourself a glass of cold orange juice after mowing the lawn. You can still smell the fresh-cut grass. Then your son yells to you from the living room as he's getting ready to leave, saying, "Dad, my laptop died on me last night, and I have a study group in a few minutes. Can I borrow your laptop for a couple of hours?" You immediately reply, "Sure, son keep it safe and have fun." You say it without any hesitation. Then you lift the cold glass of orange juice. You pause for a moment staring at the orange juice and feel the coldness of the glass against the palm of your hand. At that moment, you realize that you just loaned out your laptop without hesitation and with total peace of mind. Something that might not have been so easy to do during the old you. The new you will know that this laptop never saw your addicted days. It was a laptop that was purchased during the new you. There is nothing on that laptop that would embarrass you or your son. You then savor the cool, sweet taste of the orange juice with pure enjoyment and satisfaction.

When you create your self-defining future memory, try and use all five senses (sight, sound, taste, touch, and smell) to make it as real and as memorable as possible. Relive this memory multiple times. Really be able to feel yourself in the future. If the above example resonates with you, then use it as your own or create one that you can passionately feel. There should be a feeling of gratitude or peace or other positive emotions that come from this self-defining future memory. Write this future memory into your journal.

Now that you have your future memory written down. You'll then write a paragraph or two from the future you to the present you. Talk about how you feel so much better about yourself. You are much more in line with who you really are. You are overall just much happier about your life. These paragraphs should express gratitude towards your past self for having the motivation and the courage to create changes in your life that you now feel in your future self.

If you need motivation or an example for your letter, do a YouTube search for "Rocky, how winning is done." You'll find a 2 to 3-minute video. This video has the kind of attitude to express in your letter. You'll need to change the context from Rocky, who is talking to his son to your future self, who is talking to your present self. Also, you'll want to write your letter as if it's already been done. Additionally, since you've already achieved your goal, there should be an expression of gratitude in your letter.

This future memory and this letter from your future will be the start of your journal. Create a self-defining future memory and then write a letter using the future self as the writer to be read by your present self. Use this future memory and letter whenever you are feeling discouraged. Know that those negative emotions are only a call to action. You don't need to resist these negative emotions. Instead, accept them and know that there are activities you can immediately do to be able to realign yourself with your goal. Reliving your future memory and reading your letter is just one of the many activities you can do to create positive emotions. Allow this letter to create certainty in your mind that you will overcome and that setbacks are acceptable and to be expected. And the most important aspect is to stay consistent with RAMP.

Journal

This journal is an essential process in the recovery program. You must keep a journal. It is the same as a researcher documenting experiments. You need to do the same during your recovery. You need to keep a journal because your progress takes time, and you may not realize the progress you are making without the help of a journal. The journal does not need to be fancy, and it should not be filed with unnecessary information. It just needs to document every time you have a trigger and what you did to resolve the trigger.

Here is an example of a journal entry:

It doesn't get easier than asking yourself 6 simple questions. When, time spent, type of pornography, how far did you get with RAMP before having a slip, did you finish RAMP and describe the trigger. This entry should only take 5 minutes. The key is consistency. You need to document every time you have a trigger. At first, this will happen multiple times a day, but as you defeat the different triggers you will notice that certain triggers happen less and less. This slow but consistent progression is why consistency in journaling is so important. Once you go from daily entries to every other day and even multiple days without a trigger, you will have physical proof in the form of your journal. If you stay consistent, your journal can document the undeniable progression. Your journal will show you unequivocally that your brain is healing.

Most of the questions are self-explanatory. However, we should clarify a few of these questions:

What stage of RAMP did the slip occur:

Obviously, the goal is not to have a slip occur. However, in the beginning, this is near impossible to do, and that is fine. You should accept that in the beginning stages of this program, you will have slips despite doing RAMP. That is fine, expected and acceptable. However, even if you have a slip you must complete all of RAMP. What this question wants to document is the progression that you make with your Frontal Lobe. As you get better at using this program you will see a nice progression of being able to keep your Frontal Lobe functioning longer and longer after a trigger. In the beginning, you will have slips before even recognizing ("R") the trigger. Then after a week or two, as you get better at recognizing triggers, you will probably have slips before the action ("A"). As you progress with RAMP, you will notice that slips will occur later and later in the process till they don't happen at all. The ideal answer to this question is to say, "a slip did not occur." That is the goal. However, this will take time to accomplish.

Remember, your journal is not to record slips but to record triggers. Every trigger should be documented.

Did you finish the RAMP process:

This answer better be yes every single time. This question is used for accountability. You must stay consistent in the RAMP process. Every time you have a trigger, you are going to complete the RAMP process. There are no excuses for not completing the process. As mentioned above, if you have a slip, the brain chemicals will often make you feel relaxed, but they only mask the TROUBLED state. They do not solve them, and you are still at risk for the Downward Spiral. You must complete RAMP once it has started. NO EXCUSES! Even if you feel perfectly fine after a slip, you still need to complete RAMP. If you answer this question with a "no," you really need to refocus and recommit yourself to this program. Consistency is incredibly important in healing the mind.

Additionally, if you answer with a "no," ask yourself why, what excuses are you using to not complete RAMP? Do you tell yourself you are "too tired," or do you say, "you'll do it later but then never do?" Put these excuses in your journal. If you see a pattern as to why you are not completing RAMP, then the next time you have a trigger, try and predict the story you are going to tell yourself as to why you are not going to compete RAMP. Thinking about your excuses will be your failure prediction. By predicting your failure, you can more easily make the realization that you are failing. Seeing your future failure can motivate you to recognize the excuses and do something about them.

In the next section, we will talk about mental rehearsals. You will want to include your failure predictions in your mental rehearsals. Of course, in your rehearsal, you will overcome the failure every time. In your mental rehearsals, you can feel the fear of failing and use that fear to motivate you to overcome. By consistently overcoming your excuses during your mental rehearsals, you will then be able to transfer that mental ability to real life.

Describe Trigger:

This question has three parts to it. In describing the trigger, you should document when it started and the two parts of the trigger (the reminder of sex and your emotional state). This question is to train your subconscious mind to identify the moment a trigger happens. If your brain knows that every time it feels an accelerated heartbeat that it is consistently going to be asked, "When did this start?" it will subconsciously begin to monitor for this event. Just asking yourself to think back and note when the trigger happened will make you more sensitive to future triggers.

Next, you'll want to note what the reminder of sex was. Noting the reminder may help you see patterns. If you pass by a provocative billboard on your way home from school that consistently causes you to have triggers, you can then better prepare your mood because you know you'll be tempted.

Along with the reminder, you'll also want to document your emotional state. Doing this will help you recognize that some emotions are more prone to triggers than others. When you are feeling an emotion that tends to give you more trouble than others, you can be more determined to do what's required to change that emotion before a trigger happens. Recognizing certain emotions allows you to be proactive. You do not have to wait for a trigger to change your emotional state.

I cannot stress enough how important consistency is in this process. Journal entries must happen every time a trigger happens. And if you are unable to recognize a trigger but you know you had a slip, you still need to make your journal entry. Just note in your journal that you were unable to recognize the trigger. Then make an educated guess describe the trigger in your journal. Even if you are unable to identify the trigger, you still need to make a journal entry. As you repeatedly ask yourself the journal entry questions, your subconscious mind will begin to take note and will monitor your body without conscious effort. The subconscious is trained with consistency. Like doing RAMP for triggers, journal entries are crucial to this program. When you have a trigger, you'll be writing a journal entry. No exception and no excuses!

The journal can be written in any word processor. You may want to make it private because of the sensitive information it contains. To do this, you can use a program called "TrueCrypt." It is a free program with powerful encryption.

Or you can use a journal application on your phone and have an app locking program to password protect the journal. Some journal apps for smartphones come with a locking feature already built into the journal. Make your first entry the example above with the answers omitted. This first entry will allow you to copy and paste for future entries. If the app asks you to create a title for each journal entry, use the date and time question for the entry title. Noting the date will easily allow you to notice how often you have triggers. You will then see a nice progression of triggers happening less and less as you progress through this program.

The addiction dissipates gradually. As you stay consistent, you will notice some types of triggers stop happening while others may persist. It is a gradual process. Keeping a journal will allow you to see changes in these triggers. You'll be able to see certain emotions are no longer causing triggers, and instead, your modifying activity (which is probably turned into a habit) is now the solution to that emotion. Keeping a journal will allow you to see these changes in a more concrete form than just using your memory alone. A journal is a must because it allows you to notice these subtle changes.

Additionally, the journal will allow you to see patterns within the addiction. You may see patterns such as time of day or certain events like drinking a caffeinated drink or an alcoholic drink that assists in causing triggers. Your journal will allow you to see correlations better. If you know that after taking a test in school that there is a high probability that you will have a trigger, you can better prepare yourself to meet that trigger. You could even be proactive and start your modifying activity before the trigger even happens.

Writing something down improves your ability to remember it. Keeping a journal is a crucial tool that will allow you to know better yourself and those things that cause you TROUBLED feelings. Stay consistent with your journal and document every single trigger that you experience.

Mental Rehearsals

When you are learning a new skill, mental rehearsals can be incredibly helpful. The idea of mental rehearsal is to imagine yourself doing the process you want to learn. Athletes will do this to enhance performance. They simply imagine themselves doing the sport or activity they are training to perform. Athletes will routinely see better results when they combine physical training with mental rehearsals. [38]

A study was done to test the effectiveness of mental rehearsals and the subconscious mind. The experiment was to see if an imagined event, with the eyes closed, could cause the eyes to dilate. The subjects were asked to imagine an event in bright sun and then in low light. Using infrared light to track the pupils while the eyes were closed, they found that indeed, the pupils did dilate, although not as severe as a real-life response. It was also found that the subjects could not do this on their own with their conscious mind. However, the subjects could cause their subconscious mind to dilate their pupils using mental rehearsals (imagining the event was happening). [39]

You can do mental rehearsals with the RAMP program, as well. These mental rehearsals give you perfect control and the opportunity to have a win every time. The feeling of success gives confidence and allows the person's subconscious mind to believe that it can be done. If this is repeated many times both in the real world and in the imaginary world, you can speed up your recovery. The subconscious mind cannot tell the difference between an imagined event and a real-life event. If the subconscious mind is trained through imagination, it can produce a similar result as if the training was done in real life.

Mental rehearsals can be done with RAMP. A trigger can be imagined in your mind, and then you imagine yourself working through RAMP. After the process is done, imagine being free from the trigger. When you do this, you should be in a relatively safe place. Safe in that you will not have a slip. So, if there are other people in proximity or if you have no internet access would make the location safe for a mental rehearsal. However, you also want to be reasonably sure that you will not be interrupted during your rehearsal, which may take around 5 minutes.

To begin, you will want to be in a comfortable position, such as lying down or sitting in a chair. You will start your mental rehearsal by creating an imagined trigger, make sure to imagine both parts. Put yourself in an imagined TROUBLED state and then imagine briefly (notice the word briefly) a relatively tame sexual reminder. Maybe use a tame sexual reminder that you experience often. Then imagine having a trigger. Imagine yourself going through the recognition (the "R" in RAMP) of having a trigger. Next, imagine going through your action (the "A" in RAMP). You may want to do your action in real life. You can do your action in such a way that others around you should not notice. Then imagine yourself doing the modifying activity (the "M" in RAMP). Lastly, practice self-praise (the "P" in RAMP). Honestly, allow yourself to feel good for having done the modifying activity (even though imaginary). Feel good for having completed RAMP in the imaginary world. You'll want to share this good feeling with someone else, so imagine sending a cheerful text message with a friend. You may even want to send the text message in real life.

When we talked about your journal, we mentioned using mental rehearsals if you are not completing RAMP consistently. RAMP needs to be done every time you have a trigger. If you are not consistent in completing the RAMP process then document why you are failing. What stories or excuses are you using? Also, when are you using these excuses during the RAMP process? Most likely, it will be before accomplishing the "M" in RAMP. Doing your modifying activity is when most of the "doing" takes place. Knowing what excuses you use and when you use them will allow you to make failure predictions. When you practice your mental rehearsal, use this failure prediction in your mental rehearsal. Allow yourself to feel the fear of failing and everything that that will mean to you and your future. Recognize the excuse as just an excuse. Then allow yourself to feel a rush of motivation during your mental rehearsal. Use that rush of motivation to finish RAMP in your mind.

Just to clarify, this failure prediction is limited to completing RAMP or the RAMP process. We do not want a failure prediction for going through with a slip. We want to minimize the emotional charge of slips. Slips are to be expected, and the regret associated with slips should be ignored and replaced with immediate forgiveness. Because you have been taught to punish "bad" behavior since you were a child, this idea of immediate forgiveness will be challenging, but it is necessary to remove the emotional charge associated with slips. Remember the idea of "what we resist, persists." When it comes to failure prediction, we are limiting it only to the excuses you use that keep you from completing the RAMP process. In the RAMP process, we are shifting the focus from adult images (which has no importance) to focusing on the RAMP process and brain chemicals (which has all the importance to your addiction and recovery).

With that being said, since this is a mental rehearsal where you have perfect control, you should imagine yourself winning where no slips occur. You may even include writing in an imaginary journal during your mental rehearsal if you are not consistent with documenting triggers in your real journal. Do not record mental rehearsals in your real-life journal unless you make some sort of discovery that is worth documenting.

This exercise can be incredibly helpful because it allows you to have a win every time. [40] This will also train your Limbic System that there are better solutions to life's problems than the addiction. The Limbic System is more responsive to the subconscious mind than it is to your conscious mind, so doing mental rehearsals can be incredibly helpful in your progress. You'll want to do mental rehearsals as many times as you can. Take advantage of the fact that mental rehearsals take significantly less time to do than real-life experience. Additionally, mental rehearsals can be done more frequently than real-life experiences since you won't have to wait for an actual trigger to happen.

As you progress with RAMP, you'll experience fewer and fewer triggers. You will notice that you are only experiencing one trigger a day, and then once every couple of days. You'll want to take advantage of Mental Rehearsals so that you stay focused on completing RAMP and so that your mind has constant stimuli to create the new addiction-free neural pathways. Take advantage of the fact that you can practice mental rehearsals with triggers that seem to be more stubborn than others, especially ones that have an additional contradicting belief behind them.

Remember, the brain adapts to consistent events. Neural pathways take time to develop, and having consistent stimuli is essential for the brain to create new neural pathways. The more you use mental rehearsals, the faster you will see results. Additionally, this is an easier way to train your mind than having to wait for triggers to happen in real life. So, take advantage of this technique often during your recovery.

Exercise

Although mentioned above, exercise deserves its own little section in the recovery portion of this book. Exercise can be incredibly useful in recovery because of the positive brain chemicals it produces. [2] As mentioned above it should be considered your atomic bomb in the war to heal your Limbic System. Exercise is important because of the many ways it helps in your recovery. Exercise can be used in multiple ways during your recovery. It helps oxygenate the blood, which in turn allows your frontal lobe to function at peak performance. The increased heart rate will pump oxygenated blood into your brain and help flush out brain chemicals that have been released after a trigger. And exercise also trains your brain to then release healthy levels of feel-good chemicals after a workout, which will make Praise (the "P" in RAMP) easier to accomplish. Exercise can be a modifying activity in and of itself, or it can be combined with another modifying activity to ensure an effective result. Not least of all these benefits is the findings that exercise helps promote new neural pathways to form, which is the whole goal of this program. [41] Given these benefits, you can see why exercise is your atomic bomb. It does so much good on so many different levels.

Exercise does not need to be rigorous or lengthy. All you really need is 15 to 20 minutes of aerobic exercise to get your heart beating. Of course, if you can rigorously exercise for a longer amount of time, all the better. If you haven't exercised in a while, then start slowly. Maybe just take a walk for a few minutes and see how you feel. If you are able, jog for a bit. All we are looking for is a moderate increase in oxygenated blood, nothing drastic, just an increase in your breathing and your heart rate. When the heart and lungs increase activity then you know your brain is getting an increase in oxygen-rich blood that is going to give you all the benefits you are looking to achieve. Nothing, and I mean nothing oxygenates the blood like exercise.

After you are done exercising, really focus and enjoy the heightened brain chemicals released after exercise because this release is within a natural range and will not burn out receptors like an addiction. This natural "high" helps your brain re-establish what a healthy release of brain chemicals should be within a natural range.

If you have not exercised for a while or if you have health concerns, you may want to seek medical advice before starting an exercise program.

Meditation

The RAMP solution already includes a small moment of mediation during the "A" for Action. When you increase your breathing, you are to focus on inhaling and exhaling. Breath meditation is an easy way to calm the mind from becoming overactive and over-imaginative. This activity tells the Limbic System that it is not a life and death situation. It would be impossible to focus on deep breathing if a lion is chasing you. Calming the Limbic System will effectively tell it that the addiction is not needed.

Breath meditation is extremely simple in concept but can be somewhat challenging in practice. To start meditation, you will put yourself in a comfortable position, either sitting or lying down. If you lie, down you will want to set a timer in case you fall asleep. However, the point of meditation is not to fall asleep but to remain attentive to your surroundings. The idea of meditation is to clear your mind of thoughts. This clearing of the mind is easier said than done since thoughts can come to the mind randomly. To clear the mind of thought, you are to focus on breathing. Remember, the mind can only focus on one thing at a time. Focusing your mind on the sensation from your nose as you inhale and exhale will remove thoughts from your mind.

Of course, it is natural to lose concentration and have thoughts to enter the mind. These random thoughts are to be expected, and you are not to make yourself feel bad for these thoughts. Only observe that you are having a thought and then bring your attention back to breathing. As you learn to meditate, you will constantly have to remind your brain to focus on breathing, and that is okay. Eventually, your mind will strengthen and able to maintain focus on breathing for most of the meditation sessions. Try to meditate in 5 to 10-minute blocks. That's it.

Breath meditation is extremely simple in concept, but it can also be a challenge in practice. Overall your mind should be calmed when it is relieved of thought. That is the end goal of meditation to calm your mind. Try doing meditation right after waking up in the morning. You may have to set a second alarm if you are prone to sleeping after waking up.

Meditation can be used as a modifying activity. However, if you are trying to relieve yourself of stress, you also need to make sure that you combine meditation with an activity that is causing your stress. So, if an important test at school is coming up, you wouldn't want to use meditation alone to alleviate the stress but also studying as well. Your modifying activity would be to study for a while, and if you know you still have plenty of time to cover the information in the test, then do some breathing meditation to calm the unnecessary stress. If stress is so overwhelming that it makes it hard to study, then start with meditation and then study. Meditation is great for stress, but you still need to alleviate yourself of what is causing the stress.

Meditation can be extremely helpful when events happen that are outside of your control. Very often, events happen that we have no control over where our only option is to accept what is. Meditation can help focus the mind and let it know that even though an unwanted event happened that at this moment, everything is fine. You are still here, and eventually, your life will return to normal. Meditation lets your mind know that stress is not needed or helpful in this situation.

Again, we don't want to label unpleasant feelings as "bad." We want to welcome them, name them, and then use them as a call to action. We want to do activities that will shift our emotional state to more pleasant feelings, such as a feeling of accomplishment, satisfaction, peace, and joy. Meditation is just one tool we can do to shift our emotional state.

Affirmations

Besides mental rehearsals, you can use affirmations to train your mind. Affirmations can be used to convince yourself that a contradicting belief you have is wrong. Of course, you must really believe it is wrong but after you believe it, you can use affirmations to convince yourself subconsciously.

If you think about a contradicting belief, you probably feel that way because of repetitions you have experienced in real life. You've probably been repeating this contradicting belief in your real life for years. A way to convince your subconscious mind to accept a new belief is by using affirmations.

An effective way to use affirmations is to say them to yourself. You can also do this in the mirror, which adds another layer of believability to your subconscious mind. In that, using a mirror not only allows you to hear your words but to see yourself saying them as well. Additionally, writing your affirmation down using pen and paper is effective, as well. There should be a positive feeling associated with your affirmation, such as confidence or determination.

When you create an affirmation, you want to avoid using negative ideas. The ideas presented to the subconscious mind should be positive. So instead of saying, "I hate this addiction!" say something like, "Everyday, my mind is becoming stronger!" Or you could try, "My mind was born free, and it will die free!" You can tailor your affirmation to something that resonates with you.

An affirmation does not have to belong. Simply say, "I am strong" or "I am powerful" or "I am wonderful" or "I am capable" are all great affirmations. These types of affirmations could be boiled down to simply saying, "I am!" Saying "I am" encompasses all that is positive about you. Try the "I am" affirmation in the mirror to see how that feels.

Focusing on something positive that you believe will help you perform better and help make better decisions under stress. If you feel particularly stressed after a slip, you should do affirmations. [42] This will reduce the chances of the Downward Spiral taking effect after a stressful slip.

Affirmations are great, but they are not mission-critical. Affirmations are just an extra technique to allow yourself access to the subconscious mind. You may want to try them if you are feeling particularly down after a slip. Doing affirmations after a slip can keep you motivated to complete RAMP and avoid the downward spiral. Try affirmations and see if they help you. If you don't feel they are especially helpful, then stick with the more mission-critical parts of the program, such as completing RAMP and consistent documentation of triggers in your journal.

Sleep

Sleep should also get its own little section because of its usefulness in creating and maintaining a healthy brain. Just like your muscles need time to repair themselves if you weightlift, your brain needs downtime to create new neural pathways. It needs time to heal. It gets this time during sleep. During your waking hours, your brain is almost constantly processing information and is constantly dealing with thoughts. If you've tried the meditation exercise above, you'll see how much your brain wants to stay in thoughts while you are awake. Sleep allows your brain to relax and organize all the information that you obtained throughout the day. [43]

Sleep is going to affect your willpower. If you want to perform optimally, you will want to get adequate sleep. [43] If you are woken up by an alarm clock daily, you may want to examine if you are getting enough sleep. Naturally waking up is going to be easier on your system and more indicative if you have slept sufficiently that night. Try and sleep early enough so that you wake up naturally in the morning without an alarm clock. You may have the alarm clock on as a standby, but if you can create a sleep pattern where you wake before the alarm clock, you will be much more likely to obtain adequate sleep.

Everyone is different, and sleep or the lack thereof will affect each of us differently. Pay attention to your journal. If you consistently see "tired" as one of your TROUBLED emotions in your journal, then you need to pay attention to sleep. You'll need to focus on creating a consistent sleep pattern that allows you sufficient rest. Your body and particularly your brain, is trying to tell you that it needs sleep. The lack of sleep is one of the issues that is creating an unhealthy environment where you become susceptible to the disease of addiction.

If you are sleeping sufficiently, but you are still waking up tired, you may want to seek medical advice. You may suffer from sleep apnea or some other condition that is not allowing your brain to rest during the night. Take the necessary steps so that you can get the sleep you need to function properly and for your brain to heal.

Cold Showers

Cold showers might sound like a cliché, but it actually works. You'll want to use this in conjunction with a modifying activity. Cold showers should never be used as a modifying activity, only in conjunction with a modifying activity. Cold showers are useful in giving yourself some extra time to complete your modifying activity. If you cannot do your modifying activity right away and exercise is not an option, you could try taking a cold shower. Now again, cold showers are not a solution to a trigger; it only gives you some extra time until you can complete RAMP and do your modifying activity.

Taking a cold shower works because it causes you to hyperventilate. You should avoid hypothermia, so limit your time in the cold water. All you need is a minute or two in a cold shower to start the hyperventilation. Hyperventilation causes your blood to become super oxygenated, increasing your power to your Frontal Lobe. Also, oxygenated blood will clean out the brain chemicals released by the Limbic System.

Additionally, the Limbic System will shift gears from thinking that it needs to survive an emotion, to the need for surviving a severe drop in temperature. This drop in temperature causes a very dramatic shift in the Limbic System from surviving an emotion to surviving the cold. The cold will be the foremost problem to the Limbic System, so it will focus on getting warm, and emotions will momentarily be ignored. Again, this is only for a limited time. You still need to complete RAMP before the emotion returns, and another trigger happens.

While cold showers can be incredibly effective, do not think that a cold shower will satisfy as a modifying activity, it is only used as a temporary fix for the moment. Once your body heats up, and your trigger emotion comes back, you will again be confronted with a trigger. A cold shower will give you an hour or so of clear thinking so that you can get to your modifying activity. Do not think that cold showers are a necessity to complete RAMP. It is only there as a standby for those moments when you need a little extra time to compete RAMP.

Withdrawal

During your recovery period, you may experience withdrawals that last a few weeks, maybe up to a month. [44] During this withdrawal period, you may feel unmotivated or lack any emotion at all. This lack of emotions is normal and is a sure sign that you are dealing with an addiction. Focus your attention heavily on the "Praise and Party" part of RAMP. This "Praise and Party" may be hard to do but make a conscious effort to focus your energy on feeling achievement and feeling good. This withdrawal period is limited and eventually will go away.

Do not get discouraged; it is a really good sign. Be motivated that you are, in fact, making progress. Your mind is relearning how to function on normal levels of brain chemicals. The brain is using this withdrawal time to turn on pleasure receptors that were turned off during the addiction. While you may feel unmotivated and that you have a lack of pleasurable experiences in your life, your mind is rapidly working on reestablishing pleasure receptors. [45] You must stay consistent with the RAMP program during this limited withdrawal time. You are well on your way to reaching recovery.

Key Takeaways from Chapter 3

1. Once RAMP has started, it does not stop until each letter is completed! No excuses!

2. RAMP stands for Recognize, Action, Modify, and Praise (Party). "Recognize" when a trigger happens. Do your "Action" that includes focusing on the moment with deep breathing. Do a "modifying activity" that will satisfy the emotional state of the trigger. Focus on feeling good by "Praising" yourself for having completed RAMP. Share your positive energy with someone else, "Party."

3. Find modifying activities by thinking back at what interested you as a child. Avoid picking modifying activities that could lead to another addiction, i.e., alcohol or drugs.

4. Keep a journal to document each trigger. Tracking triggers over time will allow you to see improvements that otherwise might be overlooked. Additionally, a journal will help you see patterns in your triggers.

5. Be aware that some triggers may have contradicting beliefs behind them. Focus on not only your emotion but the belief or excuse used to justify the trigger.

6. Use mental rehearsals to create consistency within your subconscious mind. Mental rehearsals give you a controlled environment so that you can have a win against any trigger.

7. Try affirmations to create new beliefs within your subconscious mind.

8. You can take a cold shower to buy yourself some time so that you can do your modifying activity. Do not use cold showers as a modifying activity only to give yourself some extra time to complete RAMP.

9. You may experience withdrawal. This withdrawal (lack of emotions) is a normal sign that your brain is turning on pleasure receptors that have previously been turned off because of the addiction. It is only temporary.

Chapter 4: Application

Adherence to the Program

Some of you may think it is all right to have a cheat day. Cheat days, however, should be discouraged. It may be possible after you achieve recovery to have cheat days. An occasional cheat day would probably not produce DeltaFosB chemicals in your brain. However, you already know that your brain is wired for addiction. It will be far easier for you to relapse and create the addiction again in your brain than it would be for someone who has never experienced the addiction. The risk is too great to have cheat days. The brain needs consistency to create new neural pathways. Cheat days rob your mind of consistency.

You need to convince yourself that you waste too much of your creative potential by having a slip. As recommended above, you should read Chapter 11, "The Mystery of Sex Transmutation," in the book called *Think and Grow Rich* by Napoleon Hill. Focusing your sexual energy into a more worthwhile pursuit will give you much more satisfaction than what a slip or relapse can provide, even if that slip was limited to an occasional cheat day.

Ask yourself, "Have you ever had a slip and felt great afterward?" This fact is especially true for those that are religious, but even the non-religious will probably agree that they have not had a single experience of feeling uplifted emotionally after a slip. Why entertain the idea of having a cheat day?

Knowing that you have a brain that is wired for the addiction, it would be too dangerous to have cheat days. This addiction hijacks one of your most powerful emotions, which is the desire for sex. To have cheat days is to tinker with our most powerful emotion. It is not at all recommended. Do not be tempted to have cheat days.

Why Other Programs Fail

To better understand RAMP, we can compare it too failed ideas on how to quit.

Imagine the Women in Adult Material as Daughters and Mothers

In my youth, I was told to picturing the women in the adult industry as daughters and mothers. If I realized that these women had families that that idea would steer me away from the addiction through shame. While this might be helpful for someone who is not addicted, it does not help someone who is already addicted.

Just to reiterate, the Limbic System is going to overact to all negative emotions insisting that brain chemicals be used to squelch negative emotions. It will still crave the addiction even if there is an intense feeling of regret associated with the addiction. The feeling of regret will only heighten the desire for the chemical release. Additionally, turning on areas of the brain, such as shame and regret, could heighten the experience of the chemical release. These parts of the brain are not normally active during natural sexual experiences. Having a chemical release while activating unnatural areas of the brain can lead one to be even more dependent upon brain chemicals.

The idea of shaming a person from the addiction will fail. The feeling of shame has a real possibility of creating an even greater dependence upon the addiction. [2] The Downward Spiral of the addiction is a very real possibility when shame and regret are heightened within the addicted person. Avoid the ideas of punishment to discourage addiction. They only backfire with someone who is already addicted.

Quit the Addiction through Marriage

There is another idea that one could quit the addiction through marriage. This idea believes that addiction is based on a desire for sexual intercourse. While the addiction uses the brain's circuitry that is designed to reward procreation, the addiction is based on brain chemicals and not the desire for intercourse. You are not addicted because of a lack of intercourse, but because your overactive Limbic System believes brain chemicals can solve all of life's problems.

The problem is not that you have a high sex drive. The real problem is an overactive Limbic System. You need to know who the real enemy is. Even after becoming married, you will still have the cravings of the addiction, even if you are having intercourse regularly. Every time you are faced with a TROUBLED emotional state, your Limbic System will automatically crave the addiction. When you consider the Coolidge Effect, even after having intercourse, the addiction can reboot the sex drive quickly by presenting a new partner in the form of a computer screen. With the Coolidge Effect, you will lessen the time that you would normally have during sexual satiation. Regularly having intercourse will not suppress your addiction. You must make a distinction that your addiction is not based on your sex drive but for your desire for brain chemicals.

However, having a committed long-term relationship could help you if the person is a positive supporter. Having a partner will allow you to have intercourse on a more consistent basis instead of relying on wet dreams, which we will talk about shortly. Regularly having sex is a healthy activity. However, you should not think that these advantages are worth rushing out and getting married haphazardly. You became addicted on your own, and you can quit this addiction on your own.

Signing a Contract or Promising Quick Recovery

Signing a contract would be acceptable if the person is not already addicted, but for the addicted person, it is near impossible to accomplish. You cannot predict how long it will take for you to work through the DeltaFosB chemicals in your brain, and you cannot predict how long it will take you to develop new neural pathways. I gave you the timeframe of 8 months, but that is just a ballpark figure for those over 25 years old and who have been addicted for years. There are too many factors at play to be able to predict when recovery will be achieved. Signing a contract or making promises of quick recovery is a time bomb waiting to happen. If you are not creating new neural pathways to create long-lasting recovery, then you are relying on willpower, and eventually, your willpower will fail. Breaking a contract or a promise will add a tremendous amount of regret to a slip. This regret will give power to a Downward Spiral event, and you will most likely binge on the addiction as a result.

Allow yourself to take the time and effort necessary to achieve full recovery. Do not make promises to speed the process. Do not let a loved one use this as a tool for recovery. It is flawed because, again, it focusses on willpower and on punishment, which backfires with an overactive Limbic System.

A promise that would be acceptable to make is to be completely open about your recovery process with a positive supporter. Or saying that you will use the RAMP process every time you experience a trigger and that you will document every trigger in your journal. These activities take more effort than willpower to complete. Your effort is more determined by your desire to change than your willpower to resist the addiction. Promising commitment to a program rather than immediate results will be much more beneficial to you in the long run.

Using Internet Filter as a Tool to Recovery

Internet filters are good in that they limit access to inadvertently viewing adult material. [33] Internet filters are a good option, not foolproof, but an option that can be used for those that are not already addicted. Filters would be a good option for families with children. If it is understood that filters are fallible and should not be relied upon as a guarantee against adult material.

However, with the addicted person, internet filters will not work and is probably a waste of time. We are dealing with the human mind, and nothing is as clever as the human mind. The Limbic System can take control of the mind with brain chemicals. If you do not strengthen your Frontal Lobe to resist the brain chemicals, the Frontal Lobe will work with the Limbic System to experience the addiction.

If you try to use internet filters to quit the addiction, you will fail because your mind will inevitably find a way around them. No filter works 100%, and because of that, you will almost certainly find a way to access the addiction despite the filter. Additionally, the images that you can access may be a type of image that you would otherwise not view. You may develop an attraction to a certain niche of images that may be more graphic than had you not used a filter. In this way, filters can be counterproductive.

Additionally, you might end up seeking the addiction at times where you normally would not dare to do so otherwise. You may not have filters at work, and if that is your best opportunity to feed the addiction, you may experience a lack of willpower at an inopportune time and risk your career in the process. You cannot filter every computer that you will have access to use.

In the long run, it will be much easier for you to heal yourself than it would be to try and filter your internet for the rest of your life. In this modern age, the internet is here to stay, and we will have countless devices during our lifetime that will give us access. The problem is not access to the internet; the problem is an overactive Limbic System. We should focus on what truly causes addiction and work to heal ourselves so that we can become whole again.

For Those Not in a Committed Relationship/ Nocturnal Emissions

What happens when you are not having sex or masturbating? The answer is one of the best experiences you will ever have, which is a nocturnal emission (a.k.a. wet dream). Wet dreams happen when three things occur at the same time:

1. You have old sperm, which means you have not had intercourse or masturbated.
2. You fall asleep.
3. You have a sexually charged dream.

Wet dreams allow your body to release old sperm naturally. Your body is built to cycle through old sperm so that it can create and store more viable sperm. After the sperm is created, it is stored in the epididymis, more commonly known as your ball sack. If you are not having sex or masturbating, eventually, the epididymis fills with old sperm, and the body needs to release this old sperm. The body does this through wet dreams while you sleep. The frequency of wet dreams varies by the individual from 3 times a week to once a month. Most people will lose the ability to have wet dreams if they are sexually active or masturbate. [46]

Dreams are incredible. They allow a glimpse into the subconscious mind as it works through emotions and associations that we were not always aware of on the conscious level. [47] Dreams tend to work on the "what if's" of your life to analyze emotions. When it comes to wet dreams, these dreams can be incredibly powerful. Hands down, no emotion is as powerful as the desire for procreation. Wet dreams can be the most vivid dreams you will ever have. You can learn about yourself and your desires through these dreams. They can tell you what most attracts you in the female form on the subconscious level.

Since wet dreams happen outside of conscious actions, I would be surprised if any religion will deem them as anything but acceptable. Have no regret for having wet dreams. Wet dreams allow you to be free from addiction while maintaining your ability to procreate in the future.

When you have a wet dream, it is a clear sign that the body has made a dramatic shift out of the addiction. It has re-established the natural process of cycling through sperm. This event is a major win. You know you are at the finish line of recovery or extremely close to it. When this happens, it is time to celebrate. However, you don't want to stop mental rehearsals until all triggers have been eliminated.

It may take your body about a month to reestablish the ability to produce wet dreams, but once that ability has been reestablished, you will see a more consistent pattern with wet dreams.

Again, everyone is different, but after that initial month or so, you will probably experience wet dreams every week. During that month of reestablishing the ability to produce wet dreams, you may experience vasocongestion, which is commonly referred to as "blue balls." You will just have to live with this irritating pain until you begin to have wet dreams on a more consistent basis.

Creating More Vivid Dreams

You can make wet dreams even more memorable and vivid by making all your dreams more vivid and memorable. Here is a step by step process to do this:

1. Just before going to sleep, tell yourself multiple times that you are going to remember your dreams. Do this at least 6 times. This repetition speaks to your subconscious.
2. When you wake up, before even opening your eyes, try and remember a small snippet of the dream. Then work your way outwards from that snippet. Go back to the beginning of the dream and then to the end of the dream or vice versa.
3. After you've worked your way through the dream, have a pen and notepad by your bed so that you can write the dream down in a dream journal.

This simple three-step process will train your subconscious mind to remember dreams as they happen. In turn, you are causing all your dreams to become more vivid and memorable, including your wet dreams.

Lucid Dreaming is also a real possibility. After you gain the ability to activate your memory during dreams, you may then be able to activate a portion of your conscious mind and gain some control of your dreams. With lucid dreaming, you can be slightly in control in allowing a dream to last longer and control what happens in those dreams. Despite lucid dreaming, the dream that you find yourself in will be one created by your subconscious mind. You just gain minor control over the situation that your subconscious mind places you in, and you may gain some control over how long the dream lasts.

However, lucid dreaming is not required to have a wet dream. They will happen on their own. I do suggest that you develop the ability to remember dreams by using the three steps mentioned above to create more vivid and memorable dreams. If lucid dreaming is something you would like to explore, you can read the book *Lucid Dreaming: Gateway to the Inner Self* by Robert Waggoner.

Those in a Committed Relationship

You will probably find it slightly easier to quit the addiction with a partner, especially if you have a positive supporter, which we have already discussed. Even without a positive supporter, being in a relationship will help you transition to an addiction-free life easier than without one. One of the hurdles in quitting is the time where the body reestablishes the ability to produce wet dreams. There is a certain amount of physical pain that is referred to as blue balls. You can avoid this hurdle by having sex regularly. That does give you a slight advantage and will make your transition slightly easier.

Quitting the addiction will improve your sex life dramatically. Most people who quit the addiction will notice an increase in libido. [48] In most cases, other problems like a delayed orgasm or erectile dysfunction will also be solved by quitting the addiction. If you've ever rejected your partner's desire for lovemaking because of the addiction, she likely felt that you were not only rejecting lovemaking but also rejecting her. [49] This will no longer be the case after you quit the addiction. You are giving yourself more opportunities to express your love physically. Without the addiction, it will be rare if ever that you decline the opportunity to be intimate. Remember that lovemaking and intimacy do not always require an orgasm.

Even more important than the increased ability to lovemaking is creating a more powerful bond during intimacy. Given the Coolidge Effect and this addiction, it is almost undoubtedly you have had to fantasize about the addiction to achieve an erection or to achieve orgasm. This detachment from reality is very problematic for a relationship because it is extremely likely that your partner notices this detachment to the present moment. On some level, maybe even on a subconscious level, your partner knows you are not thinking about her, and the lovemaking will feel shallow and empty. Quitting the addiction will allow you to be present in the moment. This new presence will not only stimulate you but your partner as well. She will undoubtedly feel a greater connection to you and a greater commitment to her on your part. Again, this may be on a subconscious level, but the effects will be the same. Lovemaking will produce a greater bond between the two of you after quitting the addiction.

The physical changes can happen quite quickly. The erectile dysfunction and increase in libido will probably happen within a month or two. However, psychological changes may take longer as the need to fantasize about the addiction while lovemaking may take months to a year to change. However, this change does happen, especially if you make it a focus to stay present.

You should try and make a conscious effort to focus on her while lovemaking. A tip to speed the process is making more eye contact while lovemaking. Remember, the mind can only think of one thought at a time. Focusing your attention on being in the present moment and focusing your attention on her will block the mind from thinking about the addiction. Allow yourself the time to heal and stay consistent in your desires to change your thought process while lovemaking. Again, whenever you are working with the brain, consistency is key for new neuropathways to form. Also, do not tell your mind to not think about something, instead shift the focus of the mind to what you want.

Could I Become Addicted to Wet Dreams or Lovemaking

The short answer is no. The risk of addiction is dependent on the reliability of and the magnitude of brain chemicals released during an event. [2]

Wet Dreams

The main reason you will not become addicted to wet dreams is that they only happen after your epididymis fills with old sperm. The time frame will differ between individuals, but it will tend to be around once a week. You Limbic System will not be able to reliably predict when this event will happen and will not be able to form an addiction around wet dreams. The Limbic System cannot find a consistent pattern that will directly correspond to when it feels life is being threatened. It would, therefore, be impossible to create an addiction.

Lovemaking

For lovemaking with your partner, it depends on many factors such as time constraints and both of you being in the mood. Lovemaking will not happen on a completely consistent basis. Again, remember that intimacy does not always require an orgasm. So, lovemaking will also be too unreliable for your Limbic System to form an addiction around it. Additionally, when you are lovemaking, the focus is not only on you but on your partner as well. This shift in focus will also cause your Limbic System not to form an addiction around lovemaking.

Another reason why the act of lovemaking will not form an addiction is because of the Coolidge Effect. Without the introduction of a novel female, the brain reaches sexual satiation, and the refractory period takes place after sex. Meaning that the brain becomes satisfied with the sexual experience and does not immediate crave another sexual experience. Instead of craving another sexual experience, you will probably have more desire to take a nap thanks to the relaxing effect of natural levels of brain chemicals released during lovemaking.

So, in general, you do not have to worry about forming an addiction to wet dreams or lovemaking.

True Recovery

What is a true recovery? Chemically, within the brain, it could be when you no longer have a controlling level of DeltaFosB chemicals. Since we cannot measure this chemical in the brain, we should instead focus on how it feels when this chemical is gone, and the Limbic System has returned to a normal state instead of an overactive state.

A week will likely go by without having experienced a trigger. The realization that triggers are no longer happening is when a person can recognize that the Limbic System has returned to a normal state. This realization is a great feeling: a very liberating time and a time for celebration.

What happens when you do see a reminder of sex? You should feel a normal rush of excitement, but that does not turn into a situation that cannot be controlled. If you see a woman that stimulates you sexually, you can recognize the fact without having to feel the need to return to the addiction. You simply recognize it and enjoy that feeling without the need to use the addiction for further stimulation. Your mind will automatically be able to transmute that energy into something more productive, usually into one of your modifying activities. A trigger no longer happens. The desire for the addiction is no longer there to tempt you.

Could you reprogram your mind to go back to the addiction? The answer is yes, and you could reintroduce the addiction quicker than someone who has never had the addiction because your mind already knows how to set up that circuitry within the brain. However, it would take a conscious effort on your part to make that event happen. It is no longer an instantaneous event like you've experienced in the past. Simply do not go on the internet with the intent to reactivate the addiction.

The desire for sex is to be celebrated and enjoyed. This desire can help you be more outgoing and excite a passion for life. This feeling is worlds apart from what is felt while being addicted. Enjoy the rush of blood, but then be able to move on with your life. You do not have to feel guilty for feeling that rush, which is a tendency that one feels while addicted. The anxious feelings will be replaced with enjoyment because you no longer need to fear triggers.

The desire for sex and sexual intimacy is God-given. To look down upon it, would be to shun one of God's greatest gifts. Through this desire, one can create long-lasting relationships and allows for the creation of children and families. It is essential to our wellbeing.

So, if you were to stumble upon graphic images on the computer, you can give yourself a moment of pause. Allow yourself that moment of excitement but then be able to recognize it for what it is, a desire for sexual intimacy. After that recognition, you will then be able to continue with your life. No longer does it have to be something that controls you. You now have control over yourself.

Tips for Keeping a Relationship While in Recovery

There are two main ideas or beliefs that make it much easier for your partner to deal with the addiction. These two ideas are (1) that the addiction is a mental illness, and (2) that you feel remorse. [49]

Addiction as an Illness

The addiction must be viewed as a malfunction of the brain. Describing the addiction as an overactive Limbic System helps cultivate the idea that this is a mental illness. Add to that idea that for the clear majority of us, this addiction happened during our teenage youth. During a time in which the teenage brain was not fully formed and susceptible to mental illness.

The idea that this is a mental illness may help your partner take on a nurturing stance. It's hard to blame someone for being affected by an illness that, for a large part, we had no control over. For instance, if someone develops skin cancer because they went to the beach to have fun, it's hard not to have sympathy for the person. Even if the person is somewhat at fault for not putting on adequate sunscreen, the person cannot really know beforehand that their skin would be sensitive to skin cancer until after the damage has happened. The same idea applies to this addiction. A teenager has no idea how his brain will react to adult images.

While calling this an illness may be somewhat passing the buck and passing the blame. It is, in fact, based on truth. The internet allows access to these images at an incredibly young age. Given the nature of the internet, it is practically impossible not to be exposed to adult images at some point in time. In many ways, this addiction was done to you by people who would profit rather than something you did to yourself.

However, even though this was something that happened to you, the next idea will show that you are taking on the responsibility of correcting the problem.

You Feel Remorseful

You must communicate that this is not something you are proud of but, quite the opposite, that you are ashamed of your actions. While "regret" is not something we want to focus on during recovery, it is something that you should express to your partner. [49] With this feeling of remorse for this addiction, you should also stress that you are completely committed to achieving recovery. You should express certainty that you will overcome the addiction. There are no doubts that you will achieve recovery. Remember, you are not promising to quit the addiction at this very moment or putting a definite timeframe on recovery; what you are promising is a commitment to doing activities that will bring you recovery. You are promising to stay consistent with the program. You will have slips, but you are committed to completing RAMP every time you have a trigger. You are committed to documenting every trigger in your journal.

While blaming the addiction as a disease correctly points some of the blame away from you, feeling remorse and committing to change puts the responsibility to change on your shoulders. Communicating these two ideas to your partner will probably be your best chance at gaining her sympathy and, after you achiever recovery, gaining her trust.

We want to communicate these ideas because she may feel the opposite of these two ideas. Instead of it being a mental condition, she may feel that it is something you willfully participate in because you are sexually perverse. And that you are not remorseful, that this is something that you enjoy and that you have no intention to quit. Without the idea of remorse, she may believe you are willfully allowing this addiction to be more important than she is in your life. If she feels this way, it would be next to impossible for her to have a reason to have compassion. [49] However, I think we know you wouldn't have read this far in this book if those statements were true. So, communicate to her that these ideas are false.

Depending on what kind of supporter your partner will be, you may choose to tell her about your addiction after recovery has already been achieved. As the saying goes, sometimes it is easier to ask for forgiveness than to ask for permission. If you do this, you will still want to communicate the same two ideas that the addiction is a mental illness and that you took responsibility for fixing it because you felt remorse.

Do the best you can by expressing these two ideas (addiction as a disease and your remorse) to your partner. I would also suggest not to have expectations for your partner. Do not start this discussion with a certain outcome in mind. Realize that it is very likely she has no way to relate to addiction. Understand that the issues you are facing, she will probably have little to no life experiences that relate to your problem. Give her time to process these ideas. You may have to have this discussion more than once.

Medications that May Aid in Recovery

Currently, there are no drugs available for this addiction. However, studies are being done with a drug called naltrexone that does show promise. [50] Additionally, studies are being done with antidepressants, anticonvulsants and hormonal agents. While a drug may aid in the recovery in the future, they are certainly not necessary. As mentioned above, the clear majority of people who recover from addiction are "natural recoverers" who do so without any help from the medical community. [2] You were able to create this addiction on your own, and you are very capable of ending it on your own.

Relapse

After recovery, you should experience a time when cravings are not ongoing. Recovery should mean that you are not using willpower to avoid slips because you simply do not have the cravings for the addiction. However, that does not mean that you will not relapse. If you stop doing your modifying activities, which you should now call hobbies, and you're not exercising regularly, you may find yourself relapsing. The possibility of relapsing may be especially true if you have additional stress due to some new responsibility or life event.

Relapse, like slips, should be welcomed. That is easier said than done because you'll feel like you just threw away months or years of recovery out the window. But I promise you that is not the case because while you were free from cravings, this period allowed your brain to rewire itself to be addiction free. It allowed your brain to go back to its natural form. The brain knows what it's like to be in that natural state. You will find pulling yourself out of relapse to be exponentially easier than it was pulling yourself out of the addiction the first time. The brain still has most of the wiring set up. You have not wasted months of recovery if you have a relapse. Feeling remorseful because of relapse will only strengthen the relapse and may strengthen downward spiral behaviors.

You may need to do cognitive reframing to create a "positive side" to a relapse. One way to do this is to think of the relapse as a reminder that there was a good reason why you quit the addiction and this relapse is just a reminder of why you quit in the first place — saying to yourself that this relapse will only make you stronger and will make you even more determined never to return.

Another way to look at relapse is to take all the days you were free from the addiction and compare them to the days during relapse. So, let's say you were addiction-free for 6 months or 180 days. You relapsed and had 3 days of slips. Doing quick math, you could divide the addiction-free days from the total number of days: 180/183=.98 or 98%. You have been addiction free for 98% of the time. Compare that to when you were in the addiction where you were probably 50% to 0% addiction free. You have done quite well. This new perspective is cognitive reframing use it to stay positive. The idea is to make yourself focus on the wins that you have had and minimize loses so that you stay motivated and have the desire to re-engage with the program.

If you've added more stress to your life and that in turn caused a relapse, you can better predict what modifying activities you need to do to combat that new stressful situation. If you are unable to resolve the stress through modifying activities, you may want to find a way to eliminate whatever it is that added stress from your life. When you start the program again, you will not be fighting different unknown triggers. You will already know what the cause of the new stress is in your life. Or you will be fighting triggers that you've already discovered and know how to beat. This time around, it will be more of a matter of doing rather than achieving self-discovery plus the doing.

Having achieved recovery one time will make it so much easier to achieve it again. The last thing you should think about is that you have failed. You are so much better and wiser now that recovering from a relapse will be a walk in the park. It won't take you 8 months, as suggested with your original recovery. Recovery from a relapse will be more like weeks. If you were to put a date to your goal of achieving recovery after relapse, you'd probably shoot for around 3 weeks, and that would be a conservative estimate. A week may be all you need.

What you want to do if you find yourself having relapsed is to go back to the basics. Re-read this book. Start doing the things that got you out of the addiction in the first place. The faster you start regaining your sobriety, the easier it will be to burn off any DeltaFosB chemicals you have developed during relapse. Time is of the essence. You cannot waste time feeling bad for yourself. You've got to congratulate yourself on the wins that you had and know with certainty that you can do it again. And then get going and start doing.

Relapse like slips is a natural process in recovery. Each time you restart the program, it is another shot at complete recovery. [2] If the program was able to achieve months of recovery before relapse, that very same program could achieve perfect recovery with your next attempt.

It's not over until I win!

-Les Brown

Key Takeaways from Chapter 4

1. It is easier to quit forever and not have cheat days.
2. Using marriage, contracts, or internet filters to quit the addiction does not heal the mind and, therefore, will fail. Long-lasting recovery only happens by healing the brain.
3. True recovery will allow you to have control over your desires.
4. One of the best experiences you can have after beating the addiction is wet dreams. They are powerful glimpses into the subconscious mind.
5. Beating the addiction will help you better connect to your committed partner in lovemaking.
6. Because of the lack of control and consistency, you will not become addicted to wet dreams or lovemaking.
7. Please send me an email about your experience with this program at carlo@carlofreedman.com. Or join the Reddit group NoFap at http://www.reddit.com/r/NoFap/ and recommend the program to the group.

Chapter 5: Conclusion

Conclusion

You've made it to the end. Congratulations! You've worked through your excuses and made it to the end. You are a doer. I am incredibly grateful to have a small part in your recovery process. Like mentioned before, the desire and the doing is all up to you. You are the one who will beat this addiction. I am thankful for the opportunity to give you a game plan to follow.

We've talked about quite a bit. It will be hard for you to grasp everything with just one reading. So, I recommend rereading this book once a month or so during your recovery. As you work through your addiction, there will be topics in this book that will have more meaning to you as you progress through the addiction.

As I am sure you have noticed, I have repeated certain key elements of this program multiple times. Repetition was used to stress the importance of these key elements. With that being said, I have to reiterate one more time (please don't roll your eyes) the number one key to changing your brain is consistency. That is why it is stressed so heavily that "once RAMP has started, it does not stop until each letter is completed." Every time you recognize a trigger, you must complete RAMP. Even if you have a slip during the process, you still must complete RAMP. In the beginning, you may not even recognize a trigger until you've had a slip. Every slip starts with a trigger. So even if you have a slip and missed the "R" for recognizing the trigger, you still need to complete all of RAMP. There is no exception and no excuses for not completing RAMP. Often this means you'll have to make some effort. You cannot be lazy and achieve success. You must be consistent. If you've made it this far in the book, I'm sure you are a doer, and you will complete all of RAMP.

After overcoming the addiction, you may feel it was not as hard as it first appeared to be. That is because the brain wants to be addiction free. The brain was born without addiction, and its natural state is to be without addiction. It will work to make itself whole, just like if you cut yourself or if you break a bone. The body wants to be whole again, and it can heal itself back to its natural state. Your brain will do the same for you. It just needs the Limbic System to go from an enemy back to an ally, to go from being overactive to normal activity. This program, if used consistently, will calm your Limbic System back to its natural state. Once this happens, your Frontal Lobe will eliminate the unwanted neural pathway that causes the addiction and will eliminate the DeltaFosB chemicals that linger. Your brain will return to its natural state, which is to be without addiction.

I remember the moment when I realized my brain was healed. I was staring out the front window onto the street in front of my house. I then saw the light blue blinds to that window and realized I had not shut them in over a week. It was my routine before a slip to shut the blinds. Then it hit me, quite powerfully, that the reason I had not shut those blinds was due to not having a slip and even better was that there were no triggers either. I had not made a journal entry for over a week. My mind had been calmed. The addiction was over! It was a feeling I will never forget — a feeling of overwhelming joy. The years of being addicted were at an end. I now had my control back. Liberation was mine, and I was a free man once again. Now it is your turn to quit this addiction.

Please Help Others Find this Program

I hope this program was able to help you in your recovery. If you found this program beneficial, I'd like to ask for one huge favor. Please do just one of the following two options:

1. Email me your recommendation to carlo@carlofreedman.com so that I can use it to encourage others.
2. Join the Reddit group NoFap which you can find at http://www.reddit.com/r/NoFap/. Then share your experience of this program with that group. It is probably the largest community of people who are, or have, quit this addiction.
3. Share a review of this book.

You can do either of these things anonymously. It is important to help spread the word about this program. If we can get more people to use this program, we may be able to gain new insights into making this program even better with future editions. It will help this program become better for future participants.

Given the subject matter, it is unlikely that this book will be able to enjoy word of mouth recommendations. That leaves us with online recommendations, which can be done anonymously. Let the fear of ridicule be diminished with the ability to make your comment through anonymity either by email or through the Reddit group or any other website that reviews books.

As you have gone through the pain of the addiction and then achieving joy through recovery, there should be a natural inclination to help others. You can do this through a simple recommendation.

If you have any suggestions or have additional questions, I'd love to hear them at the same email address carlo@carlofreedman. com.

Damn the torpedoes, full speed ahead.

-Admiral David Farragut

Thank you!

Cheat Sheet

Here is a breakdown of the program. Let's start with a Checklist of activities you need to set up in order of importance.

1. Set up a journal. Use Microsoft Word or a journal type app on your phone. If you are concerned about privacy, make the journal password protected by using TrueCrypt for your computer or use an application locking program on your phone.
2. Then write a letter from the future self to present self.
3. Find modifying activities by thinking about your childhood and then finding the adult equivalent of that activity. Make a list and include it in your journal after your letter.
4. Copy the journal entry that is in this program and without answers so you can copy and paste for future journal entries.
5. Set up your exercise routine. Join a gym or get jogging shoes as needed.
6. Begin using mental rehearsals multiple times a day, if possible.

7. Begin breath meditations each morning, and when you are experiencing stress.
8. Begin using affirmations as needed.
9. Learn to distinguish between the feelings felt between an emotion (chemical release in the brain) and a thought (electrical release in the brain).

What to do when you experience a trigger. Start the RAMP process every time a trigger happens (once RAMP starts it doesn't stop till all 4 steps are completed):

1. Recognize that a trigger has happened.
2. Start your Action, which includes touching your thumb with another finger. Reposition your body so that you are in a position of strength, meaning head up, shoulders back, and back straight. Breathe deeply by fully expanding your lungs a dozen times, which should last for a minute. Focus your mind on the sensation of air entering your nose and leaving your nose.
3. Do your modifying activity. The activity you choose to do is tied to the trigger that you recognized. Your modifying activity should be tailored to the TROUBLED emotion that is tied to your trigger.
4. Practice "Praising" yourself. Allow yourself to feel good about completing RAMP. Focus on positive feelings that are produced by your modifying activity. Also, forgive yourself if you had a slip. Feelings of regret are to be ignored and replaced with self-praise. Also, you could double the good feelings by "Party." Party means sharing your good feelings with someone else. Always document all triggers in your journal.

Key concepts:

1. The vast majority of people with addiction can overcome addiction without any help from the medical community. They are called "natural recoverers."
2. The brain was born without addiction, and its natural state is to be without addiction. The brain will work with you to heal itself.
3. Triggers are not sins. Triggers are good because they allow you to learn about your emotional state. Each trigger is a chance to complete the RAMP system and heal your mind.
4. You are not addicted to adult images; you are addicted to brain chemicals. What we resist persists. Do not give adult images power by making them emotionally charged. Adult images have no importance in your addiction or the cure.
5. Notice your emotions. There are no bad emotions. Simply recognize "negative" emotions and then do things internally and externally to change your emotional state.
6. You have been conditioned since birth to punish bad behavior. However, with this addiction, you must immediately forgive yourself for all slips. Punishing or feeling bad for slips will not help you overcome the addiction. In fact, making yourself feel bad for slips will only reinforce the addiction. You must immediately forgive yourself.
7. Exercise can be incredibly helpful. Exercising will oxygenate your blood, which enhances your frontal lobe and cleans out brain chemicals. Additionally, it can be used as a modifying activity or combined with other modifying activity.
8. Consistency is extremely important. Every trigger should be documented in your journal, and RAMP should be completed after every trigger. Every slip starts with a trigger; even if you did not notice it, the slip occurred only after experiencing a trigger.

9. If you are in a relationship, two key concepts need to be conveyed to your partner; that the addiction is an illness and that you are remorseful.

This book will not receive tradition recommendations through word of mouth. After recovery, please take a moment to write a recommendation to carlo@carlofreedman.com or the Reddit group http://www.reddit.com/r/NoFap/

References

[1] The National Center on Addiction and Substance Abuse at Columbia University, "Adolescent Substance Use: America's #1 Public Health Problem," June 2011. [Online]. Available: http://www.casacolumbia.org/download/file/fid/850. [Accessed 15 December 2014].

[2] Harvard Medical School, "Overcoming Addiction: Paths towards recovery," Harvard Medical School, Boston, 2012.

[3] M. Downs MPH and L. Chang MD, "Men's Health Is Pornography Addictive?," [Online]. Available: http://www.webmd.com/men/features/is-pornography-addictive. [Accessed 15 December 2014].

[4] M. Diamond, "Pornography, Public Acceptance and Sex Related Crime: A Review," *International Journal of Law and Psychiatry,* vol. 33, pp. 197-199, 2010.

[5] Harvard Medical School, "Addiction in women," Harvard Health Publications, January 2010. [Online]. Available: http://www.health.harvard.edu/newsletters/Harvard_Mental_Health_Letter/2010/January/addiction-in-women. [Accessed 3 January 2015].

[6] G. Robbins, D. Powers and S. Burgess, A Wellness Way of Life, 5/e, McGraw Hill Higher Education, 2002, p. Chapter 13.

[7]   K. S. Young PsyD, "Internet Addiction: Symptoms, Evaluation, And Treatment," *Innovations in Clinical Practice,* vol. 17, 1999.

[8]   J. W. Abell, T. A. Steenbergh and M. J. Boivin, "Cyberporn Use in the Context of Religiosity," *Journal of Psychology and Theology,* no. 34, pp. 165-171, 2006.

[9]   J. Elster, "Addiction: Entries and Exits," New York, NY, Russell Sage Foundation, 1999, pp. 240-273.

[10] G. Johnson Ph.D., "Theories of Emotion," Drexel University, [Online]. Available: http://www.iep.utm.edu/emotion/. [Accessed 1 January 2015].

[11] M. Beat, "A collection of maps on religion found on the web," University of Nebraska Omaha, [Online]. Available: http://maps.unomaha.edu/Peterson/geog1000/MapLinks/ReligionMaps.html. [Accessed 12 January 2015].

[12] D. Dobbs, "Teenage Brains," National Geographic, October 2011. [Online]. Available: http://ngm.nationalgeographic.com/2011/10/teenage-brains/dobbs-text. [Accessed 20 December 2014].

[13] J. M. Grohol Psy.D., "DSM-5 Changes: Addiction, Substance-Related Disorders & Alcoholism," Psych Central, 21 May 2013. [Online]. Available: http://pro.psychcentral.com/dsm-5-changes-addiction-substance-related-disorders-alcoholism/004370.html. [Accessed 8 April 2015].

[14] B. F. Skinner, Science And Human Behavior, New York, NY: The Free Press, 1953.

[15] N. D. Volkow MD, "Drugs, Brains, and Behavior: The Science of Addiction," July 2014. [Online]. Available: http://www.drugabuse.gov/sites/default/files/soa_2014.pdf. [Accessed 15 December 2014].

[16] R. F. Baumeister, K. D. Vohs and D. M. Tice, "The strength model of self-control.[Abstract]," *Current Directions in Psychological Science,* vol. 16, no. 6, pp. 351-355, 2007.

[17] A. Cooper, Cybersex: The Dark Side of the Force: A Special Issue of the Journal Sexual Addiction and Compulsion, Philadelphia, PA: Taylor & Francis, 2000.

[18] Family Safe Media, "Pornography Statistics," Nextphase, Inc., 2014. [Online]. Available: http://www.familysafemedia.com/pornography_statistics.html. [Accessed 4 January 2015].

[19] S. B. Leavitt Ph.D., "Pain, the Limbic System, and the Triune Brain," pain-topics.org, 6 May 2010. [Online]. Available: http://updates.pain-topics.org/2010/05/pain-limbic-system-and-triune-brain.html. [Accessed 20 December 2014].

[20] G. Rodriguez-Gil MEd, "The Sense of Smell: A Powerful Sense," *reSources,* vol. 11, no. 2, pp. 1-3, 2014.

[21] G. J. Mogenson, D. L. Jones and C. Y. Yim, "From motivation to action: Functional interface between the limbic system and the motor system," *Progress in Neurobiology,* vol. 14, no. 2-3, pp. 69-97, 1980.

[22] C. Chayer MD and M. Freedman MD, "Frontal Lobe Functions," *Current Neurology and Neuroscience Reports,* vol. 1, no. 6, pp. 547-552, 2011.

[23] Mount Sinai School of Medicine, "Brain Reward Pathways," Icahn School of Medicine at Mount Sinai, [Online]. Available: http://neuroscience.mssm.edu/nestler/brainRewardpathways.html. [Accessed 17 December 2014].

[24] L. D. Kubzansky, W. B. Mendes, A. A. Appleton, J. Block and G. K. Adler, "A heartfelt response: Oxytocin and social stress," [Online]. Available: http://www.academia.edu/1329917/A_heartfelt_response_Oxytocin_and_social_stress. [Accessed 17 December 2014].

[25] Columbia Health, "Fatigue and serotonin?," Columbia University, 8 April 2014. [Online]. Available: http://goaskalice.columbia.edu/fatigue-and-serotonin. [Accessed 17 December 2014].

[26] T. H. C Kruger, P. Haake, U. Hartmann, M. Schedlowski and M. S. Exton, "Orgasm-induced prolactin secretion: feedback control of sexual drive? [Abstract]," *Neuroscience & Biobehavioral Reviews,* vol. 26, no. 1, pp. 31-44, 2002.

[27] Mount Sinai School of Medicine, "ROLE OF ΔFOSB IN THE NUCLEUS ACCUMBENS," Icahn School of Medicine at Mount Sinai, [Online]. Available: http://neuroscience.mssm. edu/nestler/deltaFosB.html. [Accessed 17 December 2014].

[28] E. L. Garland, B. Froeliger, F. Zeidan, K. Partin and M. O. Howard, "The Downward spiral of chronic pain, prescription opioid misuse, and addiction: Cognitive, affective, and neuropsychopharmacologic pathways," *Neuroscience and Biobehavioral Reviews,* vol. 37, no. 30, pp. 2597-2607, 2013.

[29] C. Farrenkopf, "Cocaine and the Brain: The Neurobiology of Addiction," Bryn Mawr College, 4 January 2008. [Online]. Available: http://www.serendip.brynmawr.edu/exchange/node/ 1704. [Accessed 17 December 2014].

[30] A. Ben-Zeév PhD, "In the Name of Love," Psychology Today, 27 June 2008. [Online]. Available: http://www.psychology-today.com/blog/in-the-name-love/200806/changing-sexual-partners-is-it-good-your-heart-and-marriage. [Accessed 18 December 2014].

[31] D. F. Fiorino, A. Coury and A. G. Phillips, "Dynamic Changes in Nucleus Accumbens Dopamine Efflux During the Coolidge Effect in Male Rats," *The Journal of Neuroscience,* vol. 17, no. 12, pp. 4849-4855, 1997.

[32] A. Schwartz PhD, "Sexuality & Sexual Problems," Center-Site.net, 5 December 2009. [Online]. Available: http://www. mentalhelp.net/poc/view_doc.php?type=doc&id=33971. [Accessed 19 December 2014].

[33] K. Skinner PhD, "Treating Pornography Addiction," Kevin Majeres, MD, 2005. [Online]. Available: http://purityispossible.

com/index.php/treating-pornography-addiction. [Accessed 19 December 2014].

[34] S. Gupta MD and E. Cohen, "Teen brain more prone to drug, alcohol damage," CNN Health, 15 November 2010. [Online]. Available: http://thechart.blogs.cnn.com/2010/11/15/teen-brain-more-prone-to-drug-alcohol-damage/. [Accessed 20 December 2014].

[35] T. Erismann and I. Kohler, Directors, *Living in a Reversed World*. [Film]. Innsbruck, Austria: University of Innsbruck, 1958.

[36] S. Lotter MA LPC, "The High Performer with a Secret Life | Portraits of Porn & Sex Addiction," The Relationship Center, 19 March 2013. [Online]. Available: http://shaunlotter.com/sexual-integrity/pornography-sexual-addiction/the-high-performer-with-a-secret-life-portraits-of-porn-sex-addiction/. [Accessed 20 December 2014].

[37] M. C. Potter, B. Wyble, C. E. Hagmann and E. S. McCourt, "Detecting meaning in RSVP at 13 ms per picture," *Attention, Perception, & Psychophysics*, vol. 76, no. 2, pp. 270-279, 2014.

[38] Y. P. David, "Teaching Athletes Visualization and Mental Imagery Skills," Penn State University, [Online]. Available: http://sites.psu.edu/mascsatest2/wp-content/uploads/sites/17619/2014/11/Visualization-Handout.pdf. [Accessed 2 June 2015].

[39] B. Laeng and U. Sulutvedt, "The Eye Pupil Adjusts to Imaginary Light [Abstract]," *Psychological Science,* vol. 25, no. 1, pp. 188-197, 2014.

[40] S. D. Williams Ph.D., "Head Games: The Use of Mental Rehearsals," Wright State University, 31 3 2013. [Online]. Available: http://www.wright.edu/~scott.williams/Leader-Letter/. [Accessed 22 December 2014].

[41] S. Wolpert, "Study Finds Exercise Enhances Neuron Growth; Findings Could Aid Research Into Helping Brain Heal From Within," UCLA (University of California, Los Angeles), 2 June 2004. [Online]. Available: http://newsroom.ucla.edu/releases/Study-Finds-Exercise-Enhances-Neuron-5226. [Accessed 4 May 2015].

[42] J. D. Creswell, J. M. Dutcher, W. M. P. Klein, P. R. Harris and J. M. Levine, "Self-Affirmation Improves Problem-Solving under Stress," *PLOS ONE*, vol. 8, no. 5, 2013.

[43] J. Ellenbogen, J. Payne and R. Stickgold, "Sleep, Learning, and Memory," Harvard Medical School, 18 December 2007. [Online]. Available: http://healthysleep.med.harvard.edu/healthy/matters/benefits-of-sleep/learning-memory. [Accessed 7 May 2015].

[44] East Tennesse State University, "What to Expect - Withdrawal Symptoms," Tennesse Intervention for Pregnant Smokers, [Online]. Available: http://www.etsu.edu/tips/education/cessation/whattoexpect.aspx. [Accessed 24 December 2014].

[45] D. J. Hanson Ph.D., "Brain Repairs Itself after Chronic Alcohol Abuse," State University of New York, [Online]. Available: http://www2.potsdam.edu/alcohol/HealthIssues/1103161617.html#.VJuEN14A8A. [Accessed 24 December 2014].

[46] State of Tennessee, "Sexual Development: Puberty and Adolescence," Tennessee Children's Cabinet, [Online]. Available: http://www.kidcentraltn.gov/article/sexual-development. [Accessed 25 December 2014].

[47] R. Stickgold Phd, "Dreams: Expert Q&A," NOVA, 30 November 2009. [Online]. Available: http://0-www.pbs.org.librus.hccs.edu/wgbh/nova/body/stickgold-dreams.html. [Accessed 25 December 2014].

[48] J. P. Schneider, "Effects of cybersex addiction on the family: Results of a survey [Abstract]," *Sexual Addiction& Compulsivity: The Journal of Treatment & Prevention,* vol. 7, no. 1-2, pp. 31-58, 2000.

[49] R. M. Bergner Ph.D. and A. J. Bridges Ph.D., "The Significance of Heavy Pornography Involvement for Romantic Partners: Research and Clinical Implications," *Journal of Sex and Marital Therapy,* vol. 28, pp. 198-206, 2002.

[50] P. S. M.-C., P. S. M., P. L. J. Q., M. a. M. N. P., M. P. Shane W. Kraus, "The American Journal of Psychiatry: Treatment of Compulsive Pornography Use With Naltrexone: A Case Report," 1 December 2015. [Online]. Available: https://doi.org/10.1176/appi.ajp.2015.15060843. [Accessed 27 1 2019].

Additional Reading Material

The Willpower Instinct: How Self-Control Works, Why It Matters, and What You Can Do to Get More of It by Kelly McGonigal PhD

Think and Grow Rich by Napoleon Hill, particularly Chapter 11: "The Mystery of Sex Transmutation"

Lucid Dreaming: Gateway to the Inner Self by Robert Waggoner

ROMANS 12:2

And be not conformed to this world: but be ye transformed by the renewing of your mind, that ye may prove what is that good, and acceptable, and perfect, will of God.

* 9 7 9 8 6 0 2 0 9 0 5 1 2 *